CINDY SHERMAN

Photographic Work 1975 – 1995

First published on the occasion of the exhibition "Cindy Sherman: Photographic Work, 1975–1995" held at the Deichtorhallen, Hamburg (25 May–30 July 1995), the Konsthall, Malmö (26 August–22 October 1995), and the Kunstmuseum, Lucerne (8 December 1995–11 February 1996).

Design of the illustration section: Cindy Sherman

CINDY SHERMAN

Photographic Work 1975 – 1995

Edited by

Zdenek Felix and Martin Schwander

With an essay by

Elisabeth Bronfen

SCHIRMER ART BOOKS

Contents

Foreword

Cindy Sherman's name has been a familiar one on the international art scene at least since the extensive exhibition of her work at the Whitney Museum of American Art in New York in 1987. It is a name associated with an unconventional and at the same time spectacular artistic procedure, with a form of role reversal that makes it possible — primarily from a feminine perspective — to convey a disturbing psychological image of humanity. Combining the roles of leading actress and director in one person, who is also responsible for stage design, costumes, and make-up, Cindy Sherman concerns herself with a variety of image-conveying materials. The use of references to older and more recent films, to fashion magazines, television, and advertising, enables the American artist to tap a rich reservoir of images, some trivial, some of great cultural significance, which she then places in a new context and deconstructs.

The present exhibition, prepared for Hamburg, Malmö and Lucerne, offers for the first time an overview of two decades of Cindy Sherman's work. The American artist uses photography exclusively, and has consistently probed and investigated its various means of depicting realities and illusions through images. But by using the illusionism of this medium, she also sheds light on the stereotypes, particularly of women, found in the mass media today, and simultaneously draws attention to the function and deeper significance of these widespread stereotypes. The importance of her work derives from the fact that she has put her finger on the pulse of today's collective and individual ideas, wishes, desires and fears. She unveils wish projections and phantasms, but also models, whose subliminal power influences the

behaviour of individuals or particular social groups. And this is precisely where her criticism begins. She refuses to recognize clichés, or even to confirm them. Her work individualizes existential experience, and — in a both sensitive and radical manner — brings a feminist point of view to bear on it.

The exhibition begins chronologically with the early black and white "Untitled Film Stills", which have almost become Cindy Sherman's hallmark. She has been producing colour photos and using photographs of larger format since 1981. In her fashion series of 1983–84, the American artist explores the conditions underlying the depiction of women, and questions the conventional ideal of beauty through a use of exaggerations and reversals. In the "Fairy Tales and Disasters", which followed in 1985–88, the first signs of far-reaching changes become evident in her work. The artist herself vanishes from the images and is replaced by dressmaker's dolls. The viewer is confronted with landscapes filled with decay, waste and maimed body parts. A contest emerges between the horror of the details and the masterliness of the composition.

The "History Portraits" and "Sex Pictures" confront both the conservatism of contemporary American society and the ambiguity of its moral concepts. Further examples of Cindy Sherman's efforts to overturn the conventions of the fashion world are seen in the unconventional work, carried out in 1993–99 and commissioned by the fashion magazine *Harper's* Bazaar and the fashion company Comme des Garçons. In her most recent work, she has discovered the world of surrealist photography, and has also begun to work with manipulated negatives.

7

The organizers of the exhibition are grateful to the artist and her gallery, Metro Pictures in New York, for their support. Without the cooperation of the numerous lenders, the exhibition would not have been possible.

We are also grateful to Elisabeth Bronfen for her vital contribution to the catalogue, and to Schirmer/ Mosel, who have produced the catalogue with their customary professionalism and precision.

Zdenek Felix
Deichtorhallen Hamburg

Sune Nordgren
Malmö Konsthall

Martin Schwander
Kunstmuseum Luzern

The Latent Horror
of Cindy Sherman's Images

Zdenek Felix

Perhaps the most notable aspect of Cindy Sherman's photographs is the peculiar power of attraction they exert on the observer. When you look at the American artist's untitled images, you experience – as when watching Hitchcock films – an intense mixture of feelings and sensations oscillating between fascination and discomfort and desire and horror. Even those who are initially attracted by the perfect staging and professional execution of the photos can hardly avoid a certain sense of confusion.

But what is the source of this attraction? The question is all the more interesting, given that some of the photos, particularly the portraits, do not seem at first glance to be in any way enigmatic. Anyone who tries to describe the images, to articulate what they represent, will not face any serious difficulties, for like all "objective" photographs, Cindy Sherman's shots contain real objects, mostly identifiable ones, and the scenarios they depict are semantically comprehensible. In the "Untitled Film Stills", for example, the female roles can be described as "film roles", and, depending on how the observer views them, can be placed in the context of one of the more or less familiar movies of the 1950s or 1960s. Similarly, models for the "History Portraits" can be found in Western art history. Some of the photos from the series "Centerfolds" are reminiscent in an ironic, distanced manner of magazines of the *Playboy* type, while there seems to be a deeper relationship between Sherman's more recent works with dolls and certain photos by Hans Bellmer.

However, the apparently comprehensible situation changes instantly when one begins to move from description to interpretation. As in the work of the Canadian photo artist Jeff Wall – whose illuminated boxes with narrative scenes often refer to the history of painting by taking motifs from Delacroix, Manet, or Hokusai and transferring them to contemporary tableaux – Cindy Sherman transforms the significance of specific topoi from the history of film and photography by manipulating the typology of images familiar in these media and the stereotypes it generates. In contrast to Jeff Wall, however, who "collages" his narrative tableaux using digital processes, and thus ultimately creates his images inside the computer, Cindy Sherman prefers to use more "theatrical" or "film" methods of arrangement, with slide projectors and coloured lighting, to achieve the required degree of alienation and suggestiveness. By using transvestism, make-up, and costumes, and by adding unexpected, shocking details, she creates an ambivalent pictorial world in her photos – a world that is illusionistic, but which opens itself to the observer's imagination all the more powerfully. Attempts to interpret her work, based on a variety of premises – structuralist, phenomenological, psychoanalytic, or feminist – obviously fail to do justice to the creative achievement of an artist who is in supreme command of every single register of complexity, and who refuses to ideologize her pictorial world.

The fact that Cindy Sherman has so far succeeded in avoiding the danger of clearly defined themes shows the ability of her work to call up a variety of cultural contexts, and to transcend the causality of time and space. The resulting sense of confusion is intensified by a choice of subjects that are aesthetically unrelated. The girls from the provinces in the maze of the big city in the "Untitled Film Stills" can arouse pity and curiosity; the vomit, blood, and mould in the "Disasters" naturally have a nauseating effect. With the "Sex Pictures", in which she uses medical prostheses and artificial limbs to construct monstrous figures, Cindy Sherman has even tackled subjects previously restricted to horror films. Jan Avgikos recently stated, with some justification, that "From series to series, from year to year, Sherman's work has met with astonishingly varied reactions", although this also can be seen to constitute "one of her most lasting and consistent characteristics". This capacity for transformation derives from the fact that it is precisely the absence of a clear "interpretation" that stirs the observer's imagination. Avgikos even suggests that the function of Sherman's work is to "reflect the observer's reactions – together with the relativizing contexts in which her art stands".

This is where we have to abandon any attempt to derive, in the way we are accustomed to in photography, an unequivocal statement, or an objective image of reality from Cindy Sherman's photographs. The world of these images is an artificial one, in the same way that television and video are artificial, for they are only a substitute for reality. In contrast, however, to the one-dimensional world of television, Cindy Sherman's images create their own context by referring to subjects that are not usually associated with art. Sex roles, androgyny, the demythologization of the body, and the changing image of women in contemporary society are only a few striking features of the loose system of references that punctuate Cindy Sherman's work and interweave with her pictorial material. Since the references are "readable" at several levels, the image usually oscillates between various potential meanings of what it represents. Depending on one's point of view, an image can be "read" psychologically, or in terms of cultural history or social criticism. Cindy Sherman toys with a variety of references, leaving the observer uncertain as to which of the potential meanings she prefers. After all, as author, director, and actress, she is in charge. But is it possible that both the contents and the topics, as well as their contexts and references, influence the artist just as much as they influence the observer?

Gilles Deleuze describes Alfred Hitchcock's films as having "visionary qualities", because in his view the famous director was particularly successful in "incorporating a mental image into the film". In contrast to an image of action, a mental image is not identical with the film's plot; it is more like a suspicion than a real image – which is why it has a visionary quality. Many of Cindy Sherman's works draw their power of attraction from this type of source. Whether it is the sense of latent threat in some of the "Untitled Film Stills", or the premonition of illness, death and crime in the "Disasters" and "Fairy Tales", whether discomfort arises when viewing the drastic images of the "Civil War" series or the monsters in the "Sex Pictures" – the latent horror of Cindy Sherman's images always seems to be subliminally present. Like Hitchcock's films, the photos conceal more than they are willing to say, which is probably one reason for their unremitting, provocative impact.

Cindy Sherman's work is not a commentary on the world. Rather, it evokes a wide range of potential comments and offers a variety of reflections, whose disturbing presence finds expression in these photographic visions.

The Outer Inner World

Martin Schwander

Any consideration of Cindy Sherman's œuvre must begin with the "Untitled Film Stills" (1977–80). These small-format black and white photographs represent the foundation stone for a life's work now including over three hundred items. In this series Cindy Sherman reconstructs fictional events in the lives of unknown women. The special quality of these staged photographs is that the artist Cindy Sherman is simultaneously also the actress, slipping chameleon-like into a wide variety of female roles. The photographs appear to be from real life – and at the same time, they recall films of the 1950s and early 1960s. This confusing interference between various levels of time and reality is central to understanding why Sherman's photographs lack an "essential" core for the observer.

Cindy Sherman has never thought it necessary to provide any theoretical foundation for the sophisticated game she plays with remembered and invented elements, with things dreamt and experienced, with high culture and popular culture, and with appearance and reality. She is said to have been shy of theory – "intellectually reticent"[1] – even as a student. Since the early 1980s, numerous critics have attempted to supply her work with a theoretical foundation. These attempts to interpret Sherman's pictorial strategy can be seen today to form a patchwork of the intellectual self-images of our time: be it from the perspective of post-structuralism and deconstruction, psychoanalysis, or feminism, Sherman's images are always seen as evidence of the correctness of whichever theoretical position is being advanced. The artist's "silence" is submerged in a discourse that seems to be in danger of cancelling itself out, in a kind of racing standstill. Sherman's sober – and at the same time sobering – comment on this state of affairs was, "I like to read these kinds of analysis because they have nothing at all to do with anything that made me produce the works concerned. Still, the fact that they exist is very interesting. They're a kind of side effect."[2]

This does not answer the question of why Cindy Sherman has never been tempted to provide a theoretical justification for her work. A theoretical foundation of this sort, particularly in the early years, would have provided an opportunity to influence the reception of her pictures. The question of Sherman's distaste for theory leads to the centre of her artistic self-image: the observer should not need to depend either on a theoretical "framework" or on explanations to understand artistic products. Sherman's declared aim is to create a post-Warhol art, a form of art to which as many people as possible can have access: "When I was at school, I got more and more annoyed by this attitude that art has to be so terribly religious or sacred, and I wanted to create something that people could relate to without having read a book about it beforehand. Something that would appeal to anybody at all; even if he didn't understand it completely, he would still be able to get something out of it. That was how I came up with culture, I wanted to imitate it and make fun of it, and that's what I actually did."[3] Cindy Sherman has remained true to this working principle to the present day. In our capitalist society, her commercial success is the best measurement of the extent to which she has achieved her goal.

Cindy Sherman belongs to the first generation of

artists who have grown up with television.[4] Against the background of this experience, artistic products can only endure if they can stand up, in the eyes of the image "consumers", to a comparison with media-generated images. From this point of view, images have to be primarily "flashy"; they have to exhibit a fine, seductive, and entertaining surface; and they have to have fetish-like qualities that cast a spell on the observer. This "spectacular" surface, which assures visual recognition, does not, however, preclude what is often an uncomfortable, uncanny "depth" in Cindy Sherman's work. At a time when strategies are (once again) being sought to release art from its self-inflicted isolation and social irrelevance, the multiple readings found in Sherman's images confer an exemplary character on her work.

II

From 1975 to 1995, Cindy Sherman produced more than ten cycles of works: the "Untitled Film Stills" (1977–80) and the "Sex Pictures" (1992) mark the two extremes of a creative development that has undergone dramatic changes since the mid-1980s. The "Sex Pictures" are meant to confront the observer in a "shocking" fashion with images of widely varying forms of sexuality. The grotesqueness and artificiality of these dramatic productions, however, are also capable of triggering laughter.

Our awareness of these more recent works alters our perception of the earlier ones – particularly of the "Untitled Film Stills". Underneath the neat surface, signs of fear and alarm, of loneliness and alienation, become noticeable in Sherman's early heroines. These signs are camouflaged by the conditioned body language of socially prescribed roles, such as housewife, student, lover or film star. Their often charming appearance contributes to the distraction of the (male) observer. This illusion, nourished by social and cultural conventions, gradually vanishes in the images Sherman has created since the beginning of the 1980s. Thus, Sherman's entire œuvre can be seen as an exploration of the myths of femininity from various perspectives – a process of explora-

tion that begins with the body's outward, physical manifestations and moves on to penetrate into its interior. Ultimately, the journey leads to a world of female phantasmagoria, in which the female subject – robbed of her identity – dissolves and simultaneously eludes the attack of the (male) gaze.

It is to Cindy Sherman's credit that she has developed a pictorial language that can manage without expressionist pathos or existentialist self-pity. Her images do not conjure up a new "essentialism" that raises any claim to thruth. The artificiality and over-staged quality of many of her more recent pictures prevents the observer from seeing an imitative representation, and thus attributing any "truth content", to her artefacts. In post-modern, anti-patriarchal discourse, this can be expressed as follows: "Let's start working with fiction and not with hypotheses or theories – for someone who writes and speaks, this would be the best way of becoming 'female'..."[5]

1 Gerald Marzorati, "Imitation of Life", *Artnews* 7 (September 1983), p. 85.
2 Paul Taylor, "Interview with Cindy Sherman", *Flash Art* 124 (October/November 1985), p. 79.
3 Sandy Nairne, *The State of the Art: Ideas and Images in the 1980s* (London, 1987), p. 132.
4 Taylor, op. cit. (note 2), p. 78.
5 Jean-François Lyotard, "Ein Einsatz in den Kämpfen der Frauen", in: Jean-François Lyotard, *Das Patchwork der Minderheiten* (Berlin, 1977), p. 65.

The Other Self of the Imagination:
Cindy Sherman's Hysterical Performance

Elisabeth Bronfen

"I don't do self-portraits", Cindy Sherman explained to Andreas Kallfelz in an interview for the journal *Wolkenkratzer*, "I always try to get as far away from myself as possible in the photographs. It could be, though, that it's precisely by doing so that I create a self-portrait, doing these totally crazy things with these characters" (1984, 49). Sherman, one of the most widely discussed contemporary American artists, thus poses a serious challenge to art and cultural critics, because, if it isn't the artist herself, then who is the woman depicted in her photos? If she does not want to create portraits of herself, then why does Sherman use her own body, distorted by costumes, make-up and props, as her main model? If it is not a question of self-representation, then what is the relationship between the depiction and the female body being represented? We must consider further, at least in relation to the work she produced up to 1991, that Sherman always staged her portraits of women as a scenario that quite self-consciously employs multiple references to American film and TV culture since the 1950s, to costume gothics and romances, science fiction and horror thrillers, film noir, melodrama, advertising and, in the "History Portraits", to classical paintings she studied at college. In view of this, one could certainly bring into play the distinction between self-portrait and self-performance, but one would immediatedly have to ask, who is staging herself here, and why?

For Sherman has also explained that she uses her photographs to reveal the latent psychological material that one does not normally see on the surface, in a subject's face or gestures, namely the material that contains the subject's imagination. At the same time, however, this other self of the imagination can only be articulated through surface appearances, through the knotting together of different self-representations. The way she tells the story of how she became a photographer characteristically revolves around this contradiction. Using as its point of departure the image of the solitary young woman we are so familiar with from Western narratives and paintings, to be more precise, the young woman who withdraws from the world, finds refuge in her own room and there occupies herself with her own fantasies behind closed doors, Cindy Sherman describes how she first felt alienated within her own family, how she later felt totally threatened existentially by the urban violence of New York City, and how, to reduce this threat, she learned to transform herself into other people, initially in her own room, then later in her studio.

She started to study her own face continually from different angles until it began to look like a stranger's face. She began to disguise herself by dressing up in different costumes, until she could no longer recognize the figure in the mirror. Her portraits were produced precisely in such moments of complete alienation, emerging from her discontent with the gender roles prescribed to her by her family and later by the conditions of her existence as a woman in a major urban centre. As such, these portraits always also articulate her sense of dissatisfaction with the expectations prevailing culture has of femininity.

In a television interview with Mark Stokes she describes how, as a child, she borrowed her mother's clothes to disguise herself, but significantly transformed herself into an ugly old woman. Embued with exactly the same gesture, her photographs are brilliant and at the same time painful parodies of the dictate imposed by media images on every American girl, namely that she should perfect her clothes, her make-up and her posture so as to imitate an apparently desirable but simultaneously unattainable model of immaculate feminine beauty. For what is crucial, Sherman chose never to represent herself as an idealized figure. Perfection, Roland Barthes poignantly argues, exalts in so far as it wipes out the distance between code and performance, between origin and result, between model and copy. Since this distance, however, is part of the human condition, Barthes concludes, "perfection, which annuls it, lies outside of anthropological limits, in supernature, where it joins the other, inferior, transgression: *more* and *less* can be generically placed in the same class, that of excess, what is *beyond* no longer differs from what is *short* of a limit; the essence of the code (perfection) has in the end the same status as what is outside the code (the monster)" (1974, 71). This is precisely the dialectic that Sherman performs in her photographs. The perfectly beautiful body and the monstrous body are shown to be mutually dependent on each other.

There is yet a further distinction that Cindy Sherman's self-portraits, which are not self-portraits, undermine, namely the difference between "performance" in aesthetic practice and "performance" in linguistic speech act theory. The latter refers to a verbal utterance that simultaneously performs the action it also describes. For Sherman presents us with a dual gesture. She stages herself in scenarios by virtue of distorting her appearance, putting on costumes, performing a masquerade. But in so doing she also points to the fact that, as a woman who grew up in a specific cultural context, she has also been performatively constructed by the discourse specific to her environment. By presenting herself other than what she is, by refashioning the media images and narratives that have influenced her self-image, she insists that the act of self-representation, as a means of expression, simultaneously always also performs the act it designates. Her explanation, "I don't do self-portraits", can thus also be understood as referring to the notion that the portraits she makes of herself function as an aesthetic "performance" of the

following utterance. The subject of the portrait has been created performatively, in fact it can only be articulated as a performance. The represented subject can, therefore, be understood as a knot, binding together the various languages that have shaped it and through which it is able to express, in a displaced and dislocated manner, its traumas, its memories, its desires and its fantasies. In addition, this represented subject performatively embodies the laws and dictates imposed upon it by the family and by society, as well as any culturally acquired image repertoire. In the course of every self-representation, the depicted subject is always also a cipher for collective wish fulfilments and anxieties; in Sherman's case, it is above all so manifestly a cipher for the way in which perfection and monstrosity are enmeshed. If one recalls that the Latin etymology of the word "monster" links this concept with that of the omen and the miracle, given that miraculous phenomena were seen as warnings of an inevitable and threatening future event, one can begin to grasp how Sherman's disturbances of the self-portrait incorporate the notion of mutability as one of their central themes. These self-representations are proleptic; they point towards something that has not yet become visible, even as they articulate the fact that although it may be non-visible, the event of the subject's demise is, nevertheless, also inescapable.

Adept in post-modern theories, Sherman thus quite consciously uses her photographs to transform herself into a representation, thereby rendering problematic the relationship between the image, the depicted body, and any citation, serving as cultural model for the representation. She stages her memories of media images and personal fantasy images, and at the same time seeks to trigger memories and fantasies in her viewers by performing her very specific understanding of this culturally given image repertoire. In so doing she draws on a rich archive of images from childhood reading, television, film, and high-gloss magazines, as well as from the entire archive of high art. Significantly she says of herself that she belongs to the first generation of American artists who have grown up with television. If post-modernist theory works on the assumption that the socialized body is always already inscribed by the image repertoire within which it finds itself emplaced, then Cindy Sherman, one could say, in turn inscribes these culturally transmitted images with the "performances" recorded in her photographs. In the process, she unsettles the relationship between authentic body and its pictorial representation, between original image and body masquerade. In her *non*-self-portraits composite images emerge, assembled from body parts and prostheses; bodies that disolve gender boundaries, that trouble the distinction between human and animal, between living body and corpse or prosthesis. At the same time she also produces hybrid bodies, given the enmeshment of model image and body performance, between memory and self-fashioning, between latent psychic material and manifest expression. "I see myself as a composite of all the things I've done", she explains (quoted in Kellein, 1991, 9).

Sherman's self-representations can thus be seen, on the one hand, as the serial fashionings of a plethora of potential identities. On the other hand, they raise the question whether this highly intricate role playing stages the represented subject as a false self, a mimicry; whether the illusion of authenticity is preserved even though such a gesture is intended to deceive; or whether beneath the surface, beneath the media composite, an autonomous self nevertheless does exist. Are we irrevocably caught up in the free-play of simulacra, or can an authentic articulation of the self emerge in the midst of post-modern simulations? Can we as spectators discern an intact subject behind the performance and in addition, can we recognize in these *non*-self-portraits a woman who is radically other than ourselves? Or are we, as Sherman at least suggests, primarily expecting to find our own self-image mirrored in the representation of this Other? "People are going to look under the make-up and wigs for that common denominator, the recognizable. I'm trying to make other people recognize something of themselves rather than me" (cited in Schulz-Hoffmann 1991, 30). Sherman thus not only addresses the hermeneutic problem that any spectator will first and foremost find him or herself, his or her memories and fantasies reflected in the image. Rather, she also points to the fact that, in

order to become meaningful, each image requires an interpretive story, regardless whether in the process the series of stills is supplemented by a narrative, or whether it is reshaped into our own fantasy scene.

By calling upon us to exercise our own memory and imagination, but doing so precisely by staging stereotypic figures — from the image repertoire of femininity, of fairy tales, or of horror films — Sherman succinctly raises the question whether the fantasies thus aroused are really authentic, or perhaps nothing more than clichés. Concomittantly she forces us to consider whether we, the spectators of the images, might not be like the represented hybrid bodies, namely the composites of a play of simulacra, as she equally asks us to consider whether in the process of spectatorship, we are able to reach that realm of the imagination that is specifically unique to each of us. In addition, by turning herself into the image and at the same time constructing this image herself, Sherman not only knots together what are otherwise separate entities — the cited media image, the model, the representation and the effect of viewing. She also stages herself as a hybrid being, oscillating between empowered subject and disempowered object of the gaze. She critically refashions the relationship of the artist to the traditional image repertoire of femininity out of which, but also against which, she designs herself. She does this by installing and as it were parodying the traditional analogy between femininity and the image, even as she performs the extent to which the femininity being represented is in fact a viewing effect, given that each still implicitly elicits an interpretive narrative to accompany it.

Craig Owens argues, "Sherman's photographs themselves function as mirror-masks that reflect back at the viewer his own desire (and the spectator posited by this work is invariably male) — specifically, the masculine desire to fix the woman in a stable and stabilizing identity... but while Sherman may pose as a pin up, she still cannot be pinned down" (1992, 183). No matter how much, therefore, we are tempted to see Sherman's photographs as a way of processing the media image repertoire that she quite explicitly sees as her artistic material, it must not be forgotten that the reason these photographs are not self-portraits in the conventional sense may be because they articulate that other, unconscious self that can only emerge in the process of staging the imagination, ie. by virtue of a displaced representation. For although in the interview with Kallfelz Sherman insists that she does not do self-portraits, she is quick to concede that her photographs do have a real psychic point of reference; "and that's the other aspect. It could be that I really do let out some crazy person inside me in this way."

Ultimately, Sherman's hybrid and composite technique aims at making manifest the way in which vulnerability and masquerade, perfection and monstrosity are enmeshed. The performance of her masked, disfigured or displaced body is meant to serve as an apotropaic gesture against, and as a reference to the body's vulnerability, to the fallibility of identity, and to anxieties about destruction and death, regardless of whether these fears have their origin in an actual experience of threatening events, or merely in childhood nightmares. While Sherman seeks to evoke memory and fantasy images in her spectators in order, on the one hand, to demythologize traditional stereotypes, especially regarding femininity, and to deconstruct the primacy of the idealized body, she seeks, on the other hand, to evoke those images of horror that are usually represssed – anxieties about fragmentation, dissolution, or the substitution of the human body with artificial body parts and prostheses. Staging a masquerade of the self serves a critical, even if displaced project. If the post-modern subject is conventionally conceived as a "network of quotations, a complete blurring of image and identity" (Bryson 1991, 98), Sherman on the one hand shows what the logical conclusion of the idealized image of the intact body, as well as the reference-free simulacrum is, i.e. the female body petrified into a mask, a prosthesis, a doll. On the other hand, she points to the realm that is foreclosed by both of these representational gestures, while nevertheless remaining a part of the visualization – the formless body mass, the abject, decay, the process of decomposition.

Her multifaceted performance of the female body thus serves to deconstruct various codes, namely traditional images of femininity, aesthetic idealization and the concept of an intact body of plenitude. Against these codes she sets the multiplicity of female identity, a collapsing of the distinction between designing an image and becoming an image, as well as images of the transcience of the body. Her photographic performance exposes what lies beneath the cosmetic surface ("Disaster Pictures", "Fairy Tales"), or reduces everything to a simulacrum ("Film Stills", "Centerfolds", "Fashion"), to anatomical body parts and prostheses ("Specimens", "Sex Pictures"). What is staged is the question, "where is the subject located, given its performative constitution through trauma, sexuality, and media images?" This performance, in turn, points to what has been foreclosed, to the traumatic material that inhabits each of us, just as it also points to the fact that our subjectivity is the result of the discursive field which has inscribed us. In lieu of self-portraits Sherman offers the knotting together of a given cultural image repertoire, with memory traces, creations of fantasy and figures of the traumatic.

*

In contrast to her earlier work, Cindy Sherman no longer appears as the model in her photographic transformation of the Grimm fairy tale "Fitcher's Bird". Her body is replaced by dolls and artificial body parts. Nevertheless, this series is perhaps the most manifest self-portrait by the artist to date. Here, too, she draws on a familiar archive of culture, the image repertoire of fairy tales, and picks out from it the story of a clever and sly girl who, after initial passivity, begins to revolt against the dictate of female obedience. She uses her curiosity as a form of self-protection, so as to act in ways that transcend gender roles. For she not only ignores the magician's prohibition to enter the room with the smallest lock and disobeys his command always to carry the magic egg with her. In this story of violence, dismemberment, and resuscitation she also carries out the act of creating artificially, an activity normally relegated to the masculine realm. Without a trace of sentimentality, the sly girl, having shed a few tears, puts back together the body parts of her dead sisters that she finds in the forbidden room. At the same time, she claims the magician's deadly power for herself. He exercised power over other people's lives by hewing intact bodies, above all those of beautiful women, into pieces and then demonstratively putting them in a cauldron, which, consciously placed in the centre of the forbidden chamber, resembles an exhibition display. In her photographic transformation of the fairy tale, Sherman stages this cauldron as the focus of a horrific display, illuminating it with a golden ray of light and placing it in front of a curtain with a skull, an iron chain and barely recognizable instruments of murder. What is then seminal to the required happy-end of the story is the fact that the girl ultimately destroys the wicked magician, this artist of dismemberment, but that apparently she can only do so by creating new body objects herself, and doing so precisely on the border between life and death.

Firstly, the dead body parts of the demonic artist's victims, with which Sherman recalls her own use of dolls, artifical body parts, and prostheses as substitutes for her own body in her recent work, are put together again by the sly girl so as to form new body units. The sisters are once again resuscitated. In the photos, however, it is still only fragments – hands, hair, nose, mouths – that are visible, as if, in contrast to the fairy tale's plot, Sherman uses her photographic language to insist on an analogy between the fragmentation of female bodies by the wicked magician and the fragmentation of the represented body as an object in any aesthetic image (#267). Secondly, the girl transforms herself into a fantasy figure, a feathered hybrid between animal and human being. In this image, too, Sherman only represents a section of the body from waist to knee, illuminated from behind. The two hands are held in front of the stomach, the left one hovering slightly above the navel while the right one almost rests on the hip bone. Some fingernails are visible through the feathers (#277). Thanks to this mimicry, the sly sister is able not only to leave the magician's house with impunity, but also to entice the evil bridegroom to his death. Significantly, she does this by creating one last time on the threshold between life and death. She decorates a

skull with flowers and jewels, and, placed on a small pedestal, she exhibits it from her window. This composite body also resembles an art display (#272, plate 75). The decorated skull becomes a dual representation. It functions as a stand-in for the sly bride, but it is also an inverted rendition of the magician's conceptual coupling of bride and corpse, given that it corresponds to the dismembered body parts of the other beautiful women he courted.

In both acts of creation – the magician's murderous performance of dismembering and displaying his brides, and the girl's self-protecting act of exchanging a substitute body, the decorated skull, for her own bodily presence – the concept bride is linked to dead body parts and to aesthetic display. If in Sherman's photographs of these brides, the feminine body appears to be inanimate – the artificial body parts of the two dismembered sisters decoratively arranged in a pattern, the feathered body of the third, in which a human form is barely recognizable – the substitute bride, the decorated skull, by contrast, gives the impression of being animate. Both bride substitutes, however, the bird-woman and the skull bride, render the boundary between what is animate and what is inanimate fluid. Upon approaching his home, the wicked bridegroom asks the bird-woman where his bride is and she tells him that she is sitting at the window waiting for him to return. "The bridegroom looked up, saw the decorated skull, thought it was his bride, and nodded to her, greeting her kindly." With this statement, the sly daughter, working with, but also against, death, introduces a death performance of her own. Her correlate site to the magician's forbidden chamber of death scenarios, where she found herself confronted with the traumatic spectacle of her dismembered sisters, is the magician's entire house. Set on fire by her father and her kinsmen, it has become the site of death for the magician himself. By emphasizing the nipple of the death artist, Sherman offers one last blurring of gender boundaries – the magician, too, is a hybrid, bearded and female (#274).

These fairy-tale photographs thus also serve to illustrate the revenge art can take. Sherman presents us with images of violence meant as an apotropaic gesture against a fatal art project, but also as a statement about the cost of artistic creativity. Art needs dead bodies, art creates dead bodies. In the images of the beautiful but dead female faces, the sisters' chopped-off heads, as well as in the decorated skull, the perfection of aesthetic idealization meets its opposite, monstrosity. The former represent the traumatic spectacle of what the sly girl found in the cauldron. As such they stand for death as the prerequisite for the masculine artists' creative act. They function as the representation of a destructive fragmentation externally imposed by an artist on his medium. The latter image, by contrast, offers an aestheticized rendition of what the sly sister sets up against this spectacle of horror, a representation of death, which stands for herself, and which constitutes her self-representation.

For "Fitcher's Bird" one can, then, isolate three aspects of the performative in Sherman's artistic practice, each thematizing how the survival of the self is coterminous with the destruction of the intact body as well as its transformation into a new body. First, the image of the sisters' dead body parts points to the concrete materials Cindy Sherman uses in her performed scenes, to the inanimate set pieces, dolls and props, but also to the iconographic bits and pieces she borrows from a collective image repertoire. On two scores the production of her photographs can, therefore, be seen as an act that consciously employs the process of assembling body parts and image fragments. Second, the image representing Fitcher's bird is a radical reference to Sherman's multifarious masquerades, to her playing with disguise, mimicry, as a screening of the self, as though she wanted to demonstrate how it is only with the help of such a strategy of displacement that she can offer herself to the view of the photographic lens. Finally, the image of the dead and deadly substitute bride is staged by Sherman as though it were a self-portrait. The face is reproduced frontally, looking, with almost impudent candour, directly at the spectator; her other self of the imagination represented by the image of a decorated skull.

But the decorated skull allows a further association to emerge, namely the report of one of Sig-

mund Freud's hysteric patients, Emmy von N., in which she told him that the night before she had had horrible dreams. She had had to lay out and decorate a number of dead people and put them in coffins, but would not put the lids on (1893–1895). The role that this hysteric ascribes to herself in the dream fantasy is that of a woman who refashions dead bodies, dresses and adorns them, indeed one could say embellishes the dead, at the same time that she also commemorates the presence of the dead amongst the living by virtue of the fact that she is compelled to leave the coffins open. If in what follows I speak of Sherman's self-representations, which are not self-portaits, as manifestations of a hysteric language of the body, I am interested in this analogy from the point of view of aesthetic strategy. Hysteria, one of the most resilient psychosomatic disturbances in the history of medicine, contintues to be a compelling issue today because it so poignantly stages the problematic interface between identity, gender and representation. One of the definitions of hysteria that is still currently used in medical discourse, according to Stavros Mentzos, describes this psychosomatic disturbance in the following manner: "Those affected by hysteria move internally (in accordance with their experience) and externally (in accordance with public appearance) into a state in which they *experience themselves as quasi-other*, and in the eyes of those around them *appear as other than they are*. They place themself into a psychic state in which their own body functions and/or psychological functions and/or character traits are experienced and appear in such a way that an (apparently) other, *a quasi-altered self-representation results*" (1980, 75). Symptoms of the hysterical tendency to experience oneself and to present oneself as other than one is are histrionic behaviour, emotional instability, over-excitability, and seductive gestures, although Mentzos is careful to qualify his definition. Expressive behaviour and heightened excitability can only be termed hysterical when the self-presentation involved "is not the spontaneous expression of a momentary experience, but rather where the inverse is true. Excitability and histrionic behaviour are chosen, and a particular scene is staged and played through as though such an experience and such a dramatic situation had in fact occurred" (92).

The term "hysteria" is taken from the Greek word for the womb (hystera), because in antiquity medical discourse was of the opinion that when the uterus became dry, it wandered all over the body in search of moisture; one day it would settle in the throat, the next in the appendix, later it would make its appearance in the breast or in the leg. This somatic cause was then retrospectively invoked when a capricious, fickle, or extremely theatrical woman showed symptoms that could not be attributed to any organic disturbance. Such a diagnosis of hysteria, of course, corresponds to the traditional image of femininity Western culture has preserved over the centuries. For it is a cultural commonplace to view the female body as an enigmatic, untamed, uncontrollable nervous systerm, as it is equally common to stereotype the feminine character as having a proclivity towards inauthenticity, imitation, deception, and mimicry, as well as toward an unrestrained and unpredictable fantasizing. Hysteria, however, was always also considered to be the language of feminine discontent with culture; the code of dissatisfaction and boredom, melancholy, world-weariness, effusive day-dreaming and narcissistic self-preoccupation, as well as the self-destructive anger with which many talented young women reacted to the constraining gender role offered to them by the bourgeois family.

Even before Sigmund Freud and Josef Breuer published their pioneering *Studies on Hysteria* in Vienna in 1895, physicians saw this psychosomatic condition as being a disorder that staged the problematic relationship between self-identity and self-presentation. Not only is it impossible to identify any organic lesions as the cause of hysterical symptoms. Each historic period also seems to show its own specific form of hysteria. Thus in the late seventeenth century the British physician Thoman Sydenham had already suggested that hysteria should be seen as a disease of imitation, given that it merely imitates other diseases without itself taking on any fixed characteristics and without abiding by the rules of anatomy. The hysterical strategy of self-expression, Mentzos concludes, is like a chamelion, making use of

the most widely differing shades of somatic disturbances and adapting itself to the style, the modes of expression, and the contents of various cultures and epochs. Since hysteria is a consequence of tensions, crises of meaning and beliefs as well as conflicts within the culture surrounding the woman or man affected by this psychosomatic disturbance, the symptoms marking the condition of hysteria in fact merely reflect the culture from which this disturbance emerges.

Psychoanalysis, in turn, shifted the medical discourse radically by insisting that hysteria above all involves the suffering from memory traces of a psychic trauma, whose origin is either unknown to the person affected, or which he or she has suppressed. While the French psychiatrist Pierre Janet calls hysteria a "malady of representation" (*maladie par représentation*), caused on the one hand by the cultural images that it imitates and on the other hand producing condensed and displaced repetitions of an original psychic disturbance (1931), Freud also introduces the notion of memory traces and ideas that have become pathogenic owing to repression. His claim is that for the hysteric certain memories retain their original quantity of affect and thus lead to the formation of symptoms precisely when there is no satisfactory abreaction of a psychic trauma. The hysteric, he repeatedly notes, is haunted by impressions that have not become free of affects and whose memory has, therefore, remained vivid. The hysteric suffers from incompletely abreacted psychic traumas, from reminiscences, and because she cannot free herself from the past, she neglects her immediate reality. However, Freud also believes to have discovered that the language of hysteria is nothing other than the articulation of unconscious imaginations which, in the course of conversion, return from their banishment into the conscious. What the hysteric symptomizes is the transformation of psychic energy into a somatic mode of expression. Freud understands the conversion undertaken by the hysteric as a symbolic transformation of psychic material into a somatic language, as the displaced staging of unconscious fantasy scenes at the material site of the body.

What is common to all these definitions is the fact that hysteria performatively stages precisely the same problematic that characterizes Cindy Sherman's displaced self-representations. The hysteric uses her body to repeat by representation an earlier trauma, and, in the course of this mimetic self-representation, she oscillates between memory and figuration, between masculine and feminine self-definition, between resuscitating what is dead, inanimate, artificial and killing off what is animate and material. With the help of her body performance – the theatrical display of intimate fantasy scenes, the simulation of various roles towards each of which she affects a *belle indifférence* – the hysteric decorates the past and draws new life from the dead. Hesitating between consciousness and trance, the hysteric uses her performances to render the concealed visible. She allows the other self of the imagination to speak. She stages the body in relation to a past trauma, to retained memory traces, whose vanishing point is death. As Georges Didi-Huberman has shown, while the hysteric articulates her discontent with the performance of gender her culture expects of her, she does so, however, by having recourse to precisely the same representations of femininity which this culture dictates to her. She imitates, represents and parodies with her own body the feminine roles celebrated in Western art – the woman possessed by demons, the day-dreamer, the seductress. Because she experiences herself and appears to others as being other than what she is, her self-representation stages the incongruity between any so-called genuine feminine being and any visualization or staging of femininity. Viewed as precisely such a strategy, the language of hysteria can, I suggest, be useful to any discussion about the way the self is constructed by representations. Because, as something goes awry in the process of imitating given cultural codes of gender identity and perpetuating the simulacrum of inscribed media images, the self that emerges proves ultimately to result as a knot formed in the context of and the conflict between traumatic psychic material and its representations. In other words, it is precisely at this interface that both the hysterical and the post-modern subject emerges.

*

To read Cindy Sherman's photographic work as a post-modern performance of hysteria involves, on the one hand an interpretation of the content of her images, given that the themes of her portraits of women are often the somatization of a wandering desire, a bodily imitation of culture and an expression of discontent with it, a malady caused by fantasy, representation and reminiscences. Repeatedly, her portraits represent the vagabonding, the boredom, the day-dreaming of the feminine subject. On the other hand, the undecidable question posed by art criticism – "Are Sherman's portraits of woman only meant as surface phenomenon, a free play of signifiers without any specific non-semiotic point of reference, or can a feminine essence, an authentic woman be discerned beneath the surface of the image?" – in fact mirrors the question posed by any hysterical self-representation. Because, owing to her somatic disorder that has no contingent organic disturbance, even as this disorder nevertheless reflects an authentic trauma, the hysteric oscillates between the critical exposure of her discontent with the identities that her culture either offers or prescribes to her, on the one hand, and the imitation of precisely this image repertoire, on the other. In hysteria, whose symptoms are so different for every epoch, what is performatively articulated, however, is not only a discontent with society's prescription of specific gender roles. Rather, at stake is also a knowledge of all the trauma that serves as the ground and vanishing point of any representational gesture. After all, the hysteric suffers as much from memory traces, whose origins she cannot determine, as she does from her need to commemorate the dead, whose graves she is compelled to leave open.

The series of photographs Cindy Sherman has been working on for almost twenty years now, all under the auspicious label "Untitled", offer us various modalities of the language of hysteria. My speculative suggestion is that they do so by enmeshing, in the gesture of a negated self-representation, the performance of her body, and later of the artificial body parts that take its place, with performance as a discursive constitution of the self. For Sherman stages herself primarily not only as an image, but also and perhaps above all as a knot of traumatic material which finds articulation owing to ideational representations in a substitute manner, namely in representations of the materiality of the body caught in the act of decomposition, or having become completely mechanical, nothing but matter, abjected flesh, plastic, wood. Possessed by memory traces, suffering from representations, her other self of the imagination oscillates between the play of simulacra, the essence of the aesthetic code of perfection, and a traumatic mass, the monstrous. Apodictically put, Sherman repeatedly stages traumatic disturbances connected to the body, as it is turned into a series of representations that themselves hysterically perform the disturbance in the image and of the image; notably a language of the body that veers ever more urgently towards the crisis of representation itself.

I would like to speak of Sherman's self-representations as a hysteric language of the body because she performs, albeit self-consciously in the way the early patients of Freud did not, the disjunction between feminine identities traditionally offered by Western culture and what feminine subjectivity "actually" is. As Laura Mulvey argues "because Sherman uses cosmetics literally as a mask she makes visible the feminine as masquerade" (1991, 142). In her first photographs, the "Untitled Film Stills", she presents reconstructions of film scenes of the 1950s and 1960s – film noir, melo, nouvelle vague – in which she quite consciously poses as the stereotypical heroine of post-war Hollywood films, indeed turns her body literally into a representation, into the prototypical signifier Woman. If we, furthermore, take into account that she was born in 1954, then we realize that the media images she cites include those representations of femininity her mother tried to identify with as she was conceiving and giving birth to her daughter. These photographs stand as the legacy of the maternal image repertoire. Reconstructing these imaginary film scenes allows her on the one hand to identify with her mother's attempt to try out the feminine roles her post-war culture offered her. But on the other hand, the scenes also represent fantasy scenes about her own origins, and as such revolve around three central questions coupling fantasies of origin

and the origin of fantasy (Laplanche and Pontalis, 1988): Where do I come from? What is my gender? What do I desire? Significantly she performs these questions in relation to the way they find their source in the fantasmatic register of her own mother.

Because Sherman pays scrupulous attention to the details in her strategy of citation, the photographs appear entirely familiar to the spectator. In an uncanny manner they thus evoke memories of films, but of films that never existed, because Sherman's photographs are quite consciously designed as pure simulacra, as authentic copies without an original. The represented subject and the representing image are identical. The disjunction between empirical woman and woman as representation is here endowed with a very special variation, given that the actual model of these photographs could potentially be other cinematic photographs, but that these are all purely invented film stills. If the classic hysteric suffers from non-abreacted reminiscences, finds herself subject to belated memory traces whose origins are unknown to her, Sherman provokes both in herself and in her viewers the analogous effect of being confronted with freely floating and overdetermined memory traces. She represents one moment from a film, captures a whole film in a single image. With every image she suggests that something is about to happen, but leaves open which event it is that is about to occur. These women, self-preoccupied, pausing in mid-sentence, hesitating in mid-action, recall the hysteric whose unsatisfied desire produces a permanent state of feverish expectations and fragile anxieties. But we, too, are drawn into the spell of momentary hesitation, of uncertainty. Arrested at the interface between memory and expectation, we too begin to dream or to anticipate hysterically.

Above all, however, in so doing, Sherman presents the other self of the imagination and of representation as a knot of given cultural representations precisely because the constructed subject is neither in reference to any one earlier representation nor in reference to herself as model, but rather the function of the act of self-representation which, once we see the "Film Stills" as a series, stages her represented body as the nodal point of multiple identities. The

21

subject appears to be wandering – to return once more to the resilient metaphor for hysteria, the uterus that has gotten unhooked – and gives body to roaming feminine desire, to inconstant feminine fantasy. This heroine does not appear to be a firmly established character but the integrational knot of curious non-integrated details, "the sum of curious particularities" (Kellein 1991, 10). That is to say, Sherman deconstructs the tradition of Western iconography, which equates Woman with the image. She discloses the performance of femininity as a fake in the gesture of the hysteric's so-called dissimulation – the hysteric woman who in her self-representations pretends to be another person, without ever fully identifying with this assumed other role.

For what Schulz-Hoffmann writes about the heroine of the "Film Stills", namely that we are presented with a woman, pretending to be someone else, but never quite getting fully into the role, so as never fully to expose either herself or the other (1991, 31), is equally applicable to the strategy of hysteria. Not only owing to the analogy that can be drawn between the hysteric's and Sherman's heroines' dissimulation and the reduction of self-expression to pure surface phenomena. But rather, because the hysterical subject can only be represented as one oscillating between various positions; hesitating between expression and imagination; appearing even as it vanishes and at the very end withholding a final residue from any self-expression, even as the trace of a residue constitutively influences the self-representation. By virtue of this hysterical gesture, Sherman self-consciously demonstrates to what extent the reality of femininity is produced by the representational medium, how the represented subject exists as a knotting of signifiers of femininity, as the integration of arbitrarily assembled details from our cultural image repertoire without any material non-semiotic referent. As Rosalind Krauss argues, the portrayed feminine subject is imagined and embodied by virtue of the function of the signifiers, and as such her identity is purely a function of the *mise en scène,* of lighting, distance and camera angle (1993).

Thus, when Sherman repeatedly insists that it is futile to seek her true identity behind the woman performed in and by the image, that there is no depth to these photographs, that beneath the surface of the photographic image no intact, authentic self can be found, she is in fact emphasizing that her identity emerges only obliquely, as the conglomerate performance of her many masquerades and displacements of the self. Here, too, one can locate an analogy with the hysterical mode of self-reproduction. For like the hysteric, Sherman articulates herself by adopting other bodies and figures, by resorting to the histrionics of different self-fashionings and a *belle indifférence* towards any one of these. After all, her works all remain untitled. Indeed when she speaks about her mode of working, the scenario of artistic creation she offers resonates with the language of Freud's hysterics. "The level of energy brought to the otherwise faked emotions, as well as the staging of my photographs, leaves me drained", she explains. "The only way I can keep objective towards the characters I'm portraying is to physically distance myself from the activity... I don't see that I'm ever completely myself except when I'm alone. I see my life as a training ground because I'm acting all the time; acting certain ways to certain people, to get things done, what I want, to have people act towards me the way I want them to" (1982, cited in Stockebrand 1985).

While Laura Mulvey argues that in the "Films Stills" "each of the women is Sherman herself, simultaneously artist and model, transformed chameleon-like into a glossary of pose, gesture, and facial expressions" (137), Judith Williamson opposes such an essentialist interpretation. She suggests instead that because Sherman offers a lexicon of represented feminine identities, each image calls upon the viewer to construct the inextricability of femininity and the image, the enmeshment of femininity as a phantasy projection onto any single image and the depiction of a woman concretely given figure to by any single image. Sherman's work is neither exclusively a witty parody of media images of femininity, a deconstruction of the supremacy of the simulacrum, nor merely a series of self-portraits in a search for identity; "the two are completely mixed up, as are the imagery and experience of femininity for all of us ... femininity is trapped in the image – but the viewer is snared too" (106).

Where the classic hysteric, rather more disempowered by than in control of her strategy, performs femininity as a symptom without any clear lesion, Sherman self-consciously and self-controlled elicits the false search for a real, coherent, homogeneous identity. She performs a *maladie par représentation*, rather than becoming its victim, as is the case of the hysteric, even as she also has recourse to the undecidable interchange between surface and essence. As Williamson puts it, Sherman's photographs are to be understood as a "surface which suggests nothing but itself, and yet in so far as it suggests there is something behind it, prevents us from considering it as a surface" (1983, 102). By virtue of the fact that her photographs turn the viewer into an accomplice, in an act that constructs the represented woman as an image, the ideology inherent in this aesthetic act is disclosed.

Clearly we should question any univocal allegorical reading of Sherman's work, such as that offered by Arthur Danto, who reads the "Film Stills" as a representation of the essential Woman, eternally the same in the midst of all her guises: "The Girl is an allegory for something deeper and darker, in the mythic unconscious of everyone, regardless of sex. For The Girl is the contemporary realization of the Fair Princess in the Far Tower, the red-clad child in the wolf-haunted woods, the witch-sought Innocent lost in trackless forest, Dorothy and Snow-White and The Littlest Revel in a universe of scary things. Each of the stills is about the Girl in Trouble, but in the aggregate they touch the myth we each carry out of childhood, of danger, love, and security that defines the human condition where the wild things are" (1990, 14). By thus interpreting the represented woman as a cipher for universal characteristics of the masculine psyche, Danto has been taken in by Sherman's hysterical performance, because he thereby enacts precisely what she is trying to demythify. Above all, however, such an interpretation deflects the disturbance that emerges from Sherman's deconstructive staging of stereotypes of femininity, by transforming this unsettling gesture into a stabilizing tropic reading. Such an allegorizing interpretation is blind to precisely the critical moment in Sherman's work, namely the way

in which she performs the disjunction between ideational notions of the self, self-representation and identity.

Instead I would argue that works from the series "Film Stills", "Rear-Screen Projections", "Centerfolds", and "Fashion" produce an effect of uncanny and irritating recognition that elicits a gesture of counter-direction. They seem to call for an interpretative oscillation between the desire to integrate the free-floating signifiers into a narrative that would once again mitigate the sense of disturbance evoked by the images precisely by having recourse to metaphors of danger, desire or fantasizing. At the same time, however, they force upon the viewer a recognition that the engendered composite is inhabited by an internal dissolution, by the traumatic psychic material as well as the real body as the ground and vanishing point of any representation and its interpretation. These photographs perform the fact that to be subject to representation means neither an image-produced falsification of the represented self (signifier without signified) nor an identity between image and self (transparency between signifier and signified) but rather the production of a knotted subject that in one and the same gesture is conscious of the fact that it is represented as it is aware of the dissolution inherent in any image representing it; a hysterical, post-modern subject which articulates itself precisely in the interface between monstrous, formless materiality beneath the surface of the image and an outward appearance of perfection, the coherence of any aesthetic object.

This counter-directional gesture, this oscillation between integration and dissolution, sublimation and desublimation of aesthetic coherence, is no longer merely the privileged subject, but rather transforms into the privileged strategy itself in the later photographs, the "Disasters", "Fairy Tales" and "Sex Pictures". While the protagonists in the "Film Stills", "Rear-Screen Projections", "Centerfolds" and "Fashions" depict, in a variety of ways, the hysterical body performing a *maladie par représentation*, this hysterical body nevertheless remained intact within the frame of the representation. The displacement and dissolution of the subject here took place, as

23

Rosalind Krauss argues, primarily by virtue of the photographic medium – the lighting, the depth of field, the grain, the cadrage. In the later works, by contrast, the subject fades almost completely from the field of vision, disfigured into monstrous body shapes or cut up into body fragments. It is reduced to a gaze without any reference point (#167 and #175), or appears only by virtue of the objects that metonymically refer to the absent subject (#168 and #170). In these representations, the hysterical body appears wounded, fractured, dissolving. It is often absent, replaced by or supplemented with prostheses. In Mulvey's words, we are shown "a monstrous otherness behind the cosmetic facade" (144).

At the same time, these photographs make manifest what had been implicit in Sherman's earlier demythification of cultural images of femininity; the conflation between the depiciton of the disintegrating feminine body and a disintegration of the cohesive formal organization of the photographic image. These photographs self-reflexively stage phantasy scenes of bodily fragmentation as an aesthetic principle, and as such they form the horrific inversion of the earlier scenes, in which, analogous to the hysterical self-performance, an illness by representation was staged. For what is now being performed is the malady aroused by a traumatic knowledge of one's own mutability, transformation and decay. The represented monstrosity inundates the aesthetic coherence of the image and turns idealized perfection inside out. Both the represented body, as well as the strategy of representation seem to be caught up in a movement of desublimation, of dissolving, of disseminating. In so doing these photographs elicit a different kind of hysterization in the viewer, now no longer in relation to assimilated memory traces without origins, but rather in relation to the viewer's own anxieties about fragmentation and dying.

Thus, two modalities of a language of hysteria emerge in Cindy Sherman's work. On the one hand, her photographs stage the hysteric's proclivity to extravagant fantasy, daydreaming, self-preoccupation, as the thematic subject of the "Film Stills" and "Centerfolds". Here we, as viewers, are placed outside the scene, permitted to watch the self-contained, seductive, dreaming, psychically and physically vagabonding heroine, as she appears to be tormented by anxiety, engrossed in her desires, consumed by her anticipations (#2, #6, #52, #48, #85, #93). We gaze at her from outside, as she is caught in the act of fantasizing something, whose content, however, in the fashion of the true narcissist, she keeps to herself. What is staged here is the gesture of dreaming, while we are forced to use our interpretation to come up with the content of these fantasies. In the "Disasters", "Fairy Tales" and "Sex Pictures", this relationship is reversed. Owing to the fact that the subject of the image we have been identifying with has begun to fade, we ourselves partake of the scene of fantasy and are no longer excluded from its content. We do not see the dreamer, rather we have entered into the realm of her fantasy space. We are now presented with the intimate drama we were only able to guess at in the earlier photographs. We are directly drawn into the intimate spectacle, the other self of the imagination. One could say, we are now asked to look into the evil magician's cauldron, and, much like the sly sister in "Fitcher's Bird", we are not spared the horrific sight it contains – the dismemberment of the body, the monstrous dissolution of the self, the fantastic composites that create hybrid creatures.

On the other hand, Sherman repeatedly displays the hysteric's oscillation between fixed identity positions. According to psychoanalytic theory, the hysteric defines herself in relation to a figure of paternal authority by constantly renegotiating her relationship to this Other. In dialogue with the representative of paternal alterity, she constantly re-poses the question, "what am I?" in relation to my gender and in relation to the contingency of my existence. Sherman's work performs a similar strategy of self-interrogation as a means of self-fashioning, though here it is quite specifically the spectator, who serves as representative of the patriarchal code. For the photographs are constructed in such a way as to implicitly draw the viewer into the exchange, indeed this implied viewer serves as the Other to whom the staged interrogation of identity is addressed. In the "Centerfolds" and the "Color Tests", we find the classic hysteric indecision "am I feminine or masculine?" (#103 and #112);

in the "Film Stills", the "Rear-Screen Projections" and "Fashions", the question "do I exist or am I the mere repetition of an image?" (#56); in the "Disasters" and "Fairy Tales", the questions "am I human or animal, human or fantasy creature?" (#140 and #146), "do I exist as an animate body or do I negate my existence through inanimation?" (#91 and #173), "am I human or model, doll, prosthesis?" (#264).

Norman Bryson has poignantly described the transition within Cindy Sherman's work as that from the conventional post-modern notion that "all is representation" to a reformulation that privileges "the body as horror"; from a notion that the simulacrum is the only reality we have to the breakdown of the simulacrum into a body of disaster (1993, 217). It is in the counter-directional gesture so typical of the language of hysteria, namely the gesture of hesitating between two diametrically opposed registers – that of pure representation and that of horror – that I want to locate the common denominator of all Cindy Sherman's work. In her early series, the heroine, composed of citations from invented film stills, advertising and pornographic images, functions as a serial display of stereotypes of femininity perpetrated by the image repertoire of Western culture. Sherman here not only stages a vulnerable, precarious, hesitant, vagabonding and seductive feminine protagonist. Rather, the performance itself aims at highlighting the exclusively semiotic quality of this photographic subject. In her later work, Sherman turns surface beauty inside out to reveal human mutability, the decomposed, vulnerable body and the monstrosity that is inherent to any aesthetically coherent image, its ground and vanishing point, meant to remain occluded by the perfection of sublimation. Now, her performance aims precisely at making manifest what is excluded from and foreclosed by the representation, the alterity that crosses cultural constructions of femininity with the real.

I want to call this aesthetic strategy the language of hysteria because it doubles the dissolution of the represented subject by offering a threat to the coherence of representation itself. However, what is privileged is neither the sublimation performed by representation (perfection as the essence of the code), nor a desublimating disturbance of the image (the monstrous situated outside the code). Rather, we have an oscillation between the two. Sherman traces two modalities of feminine self-representation within the discursive formulations of Western cultural practices, thereby transforming representation into performance. On the one hand, there is the simulacrum heroine, who functions as a knot of traditional images of femininity; Woman as a fetish, as a seemingly integrated body symptom, uncannily screening the truth of human vulnerability and contingency. On the other hand, there is the feminine body as representative for denavelling and mutability, for those moments of bodily castration that are irrevocably inscribed into all human existence beyond gender. The disgusting fragments of the body, the abject body fluids stand in for that real which can never be entirely captured within the frame of aesthetic coherence. As the logical conclusion of her trajectory into the interiority of the body and into scenes of the body's woundings, Sherman, in "Specimens" and "Sex Pictures", takes leave of the human body completely, only to replace it with dolls and anatomical figures. In so doing she seems to deconstruct once more certain tacit presuppositions about gender and the body that continue to be so dear to our culture. For aren't dolls the artificial bodies given to girls, so that, by playing with them, they might learn the power of feminine masquerade? And aren't anatomical figures the plastic reconstructions, given to the medical students, so that, by probing into them, they might explore the secrets of the human body that lie beneath the skin?

*

Cindy Sherman's photographs, all labelled "Untitled", urge us to endow them with a title, to bind them into narratives. But like the case histories of the hysterics, so disconcerting and at the same time so heuristically stimulating to the analyst Freud, to whom they were addressed, precisely because he was incapable of finding any solution to them, this series, too, is interminable. Of the "Film Stills", Sherman says "What I was trying to do was to make

25

people make up stories about the character so they could imagine a whole film, perhaps based around that character." By forcing us, however, to invent narratives for her images, she hystericizes us. Like her, we are haunted by representations that remind us of familiar images, even as they always miss their mark. Like her, we are possessed by memory traces that have no clear origin. Her performance of femininity, of the monstrous, and ultimately of the mechanical body, compels us to see this staging as a performance. In one and the same gesture she urges us to focus both on the process of figuration and on the traumatic material that is screened out by any aesthetic figuration, or, if it can't be contained, that emerges from it in its excessive, monstrous shape. If the starting-point of her self-displacements was her sense of dislocation and alienation in her home, its end-point is the fact that her photographs have the same effect on us. We, too, begin to feel uncannily dislocated in our own image repertoire, in the fantasy scenes transmitted to us by the media, and the protective fantasies we use to give coherent meaning to our contingent existence. If in her self-portraits, which are not self-portraits, Sherman articulates her discontent with culture, her performance of this dissatisfaction consists precisely in making this discomfort disturbingly our own.

In the television interview with Mark Stokes, Cindy Sherman describes how she at first dismissed the suggestion, made to her by a doctoral student, that her entire work was one long confrontation with death, but upon reflection recognized that her interest in horror films, in artificial body parts, as well as in fairy tales, could indeed be understood in this way, since these representations allow her to prepare herself for the potential incursion of violence and death. "I don't know why, I think of death perhaps every day, but maybe it's living in Manhatten, and reading the paper, and thinking how it can happen at any moment...there are so many variables", she explains. "I think what's fascinating is that you are never prepared for it. And I'm not exactly afraid to die, once you're dead, what is there to be afraid of? It's just the unknown, and I think that is what's triggered in the films that I like, and somehow, I guess, I try to come to terms with it in my work, somehow." All of Sherman's work, one could say, revolves around staging this hesitation, this "somehow". It performatively transforms her sense of being haunted by nightmares, memory traces and inherited representations into renditions of a coherent photographic subject. Yet at every turn she makes sure that one never loses sight of the underlying trauma.

Bibliography

Barthes, Roland (1974). *S/Z*. New York: Hill and Wang.

Brüder Grimm (1819). *Kinder- und Hausmärchen*. Munich: Winkler.

Bryson, Norman (1991). "The Ideal and the Abject: Cindy Sherman's historical Portraits". *Parkett 29*.

Danto, Arthur C. (1990). "Photography and Performance. Cindy Sherman's Stills". *Cindy Sherman: Untitled Film Stills*. New York: Rizzoli.

Didi-Huberman, Georges (1982). *Invention de l'hystérie. Charcot et l'iconographie photographique de la Salpêtrière*. Paris: Macula.

Foucault, Michel (1961). *Histoire de la folie*. Paris: Gallimard.

Freud, Sigmund and Josef Breuer (1895). "Studies on Hysteria". *Standard Edition II*. London: Hogarth Press (1955).

Janet, Pierre (3rd ed., 1931). *L'Etat mental des hystériques*. Paris.

Kallfelz, Andreas (1984). "Cindy Sherman: 'Ich mache keine Selbstporträts'". *Wolkenkratzer Art Journal 4*.

Kellein, Thomas (1991). "Wie schwierig sind Portraits? Wie schwierig sind die Menschen!" *Cindy Sherman*. Basle: Cantz.

Krauss, Rosalind (1993). *Cindy Sherman. Arbeiten von 1975 bis 1993*. Munich: Schirmer/Mosel.

Kristeva, Julia (1980). *Pouvoirs de l'horreur. Essai sur l'abjection*. Paris: Seuil.

Laplanche, J. and J.-B. Pontalis (1988). *The Language of Psychoanalysis*. London: Karnac Books.

Mentzos, Stavros (1980). *Hysterie. Zur Psychodynamik unbewusster Inszenierungen*. Frankfurt am Main: Fischer.

Mulvey, Laura (1991). "A Phantasmagoria of the Female Body: the Work of Cindy Sherman". *New Left Review 188*.

Owens, Craig (1992). *Beyond Recognition: Representation, Power, and Culture*. Berkeley: University of California Press.

Schulz-Hoffmann, Carla (1991). "Cindy Sherman – Kommentare zur hehren Kunst und zum banalen Leben". *Cindy Sherman*. Basle: Cantz.

Stockebrand, Marianne (1985). *Cindy Sherman*. Photographien. Münster: Westfälischer Kunstverein.

Williamson, Judith (1983). "Images of 'Woman': The Photographs of Cindy Sherman." *Screen 23.6*.

Plates

1 Untitled, D, 1975
50,8 x 40,6 cm

2 Untitled Film Still, #16, 1978
25,4 x 20,3 cm

3 Untitled Film Still, #8, 1978
20,3 x 25,4 cm

4 Untitled Film Still, #21, 1978
20,3 x 25,4 cm

5 Untitled Film Still, #44, 1979
20,3 x 25,4 cm

6 Untitled Film Still, #7, 1978
25,4 x 20,3 cm

7 Untitled Film Still, #5, 1977
20,3 x 25,4 cm

8 Untitled Film Still, #34, 1979
25,4 x 20,3 cm

9 Untitled, A, 1975
50,8 x 40,6 cm

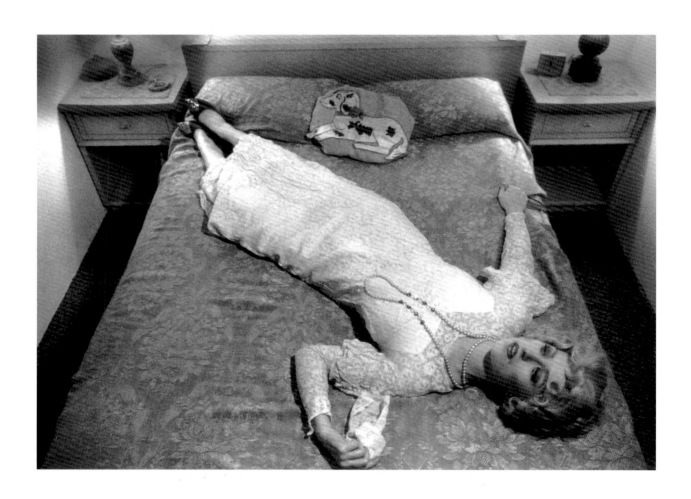

10 Untitled Film Still, #11, 1978
20,3 x 25,4 cm

11 **Untitled Film Still, #35, 1979**
25,4 x 20,3 cm

12 Untitled Film Still, #46, 1979
20,3 x 25,4 cm

13 **Untitled Film Still, #2, 1977**
25,4 x 20,3 cm

14 Untitled Film Still, #43, 1979
20.3 x 25.4 cm

15 Untitled Film Still, #15, 1978
25,4 x 20,3 cm

16 **Untitled Film Still, #27, 1979**
25,4 x 20,3 cm

17 Untitled Film Still, #32, 1979
20,3 x 25,4 cm

18 Untitled Film Still, #39, 1979
25,4 x 20,3 cm

19 Untitled, C, 1975
50,8 x 40,6 cm

20 Untitled Film Still, #9, 1978
20,3 x 25,4 cm

21 Untitled Film Still, #14, 1978
25,4 x 20,3 cm

22 Untitled Film Still, #6, 1977
25,4 x 20,3 cm

23 Untitled Film Still, #10, 1978
20,3 x 25,4 cm

24 Untitled Film Still, #56, 1980
20,3 x 25,4 cm

25 Untitled Film Still, #38, 1979
25,4 x 20,3 cm

26 Untitled Film Still, #13, 1978
25,4 x 20,3 cm

27 Untitled, B, 1975
50,8 x 40,6 cm

28 Untitled Film Still, #50, 1979
20,3 x 25,4 cm

29 Untitled Film Still, #3, 1977
20,3 x 25,4 cm

30 Untitled Film Still, #54, 1980
20,3 x 25,4 cm

31 Untitled Film Still, #4, 1977
20,3 x 25,4 cm

32 Untitled Film Still, #30, 1979
20,3 x 25,4 cm

33 Untitled Film Still, #48, 1979
20,3 x 25,4 cm

34 Untitled, #66, 1980
50,8 x 61 cm

35 Untitled, #69, 1980
50,8 x 61 cm

36 Untitled, #70, 1980
50,8 x 61 cm

37 Untitled, #74, 1980
50,8 x 61 cm

38 Untitled, #88, 1981
61 x 122 cm

39 Untitled, #86, 1981
61 x 122 cm

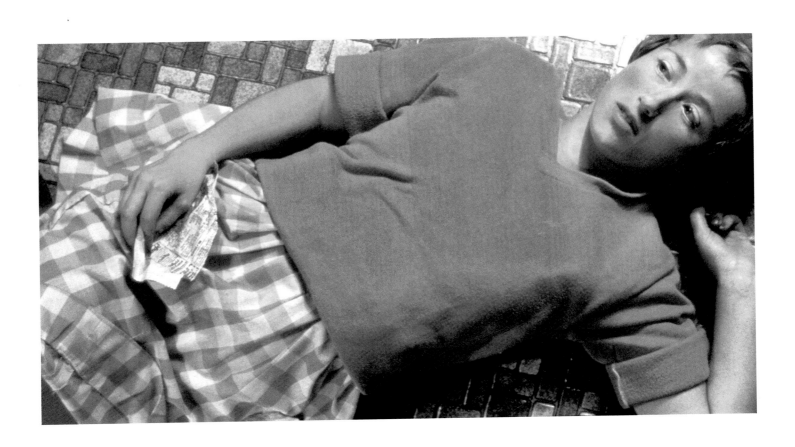

40 Untitled, #96, 1981
61 x 122 cm

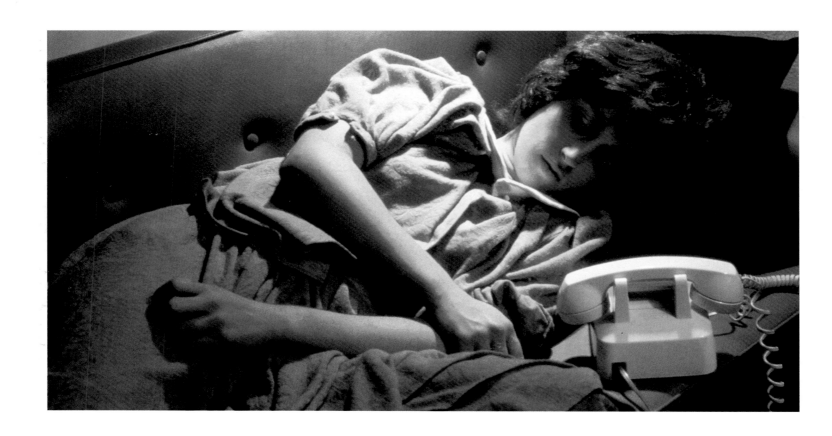

41 Untitled, #90, 1981
61 x 122 cm

42 Untitled, #93, 1981
61 x 122 cm

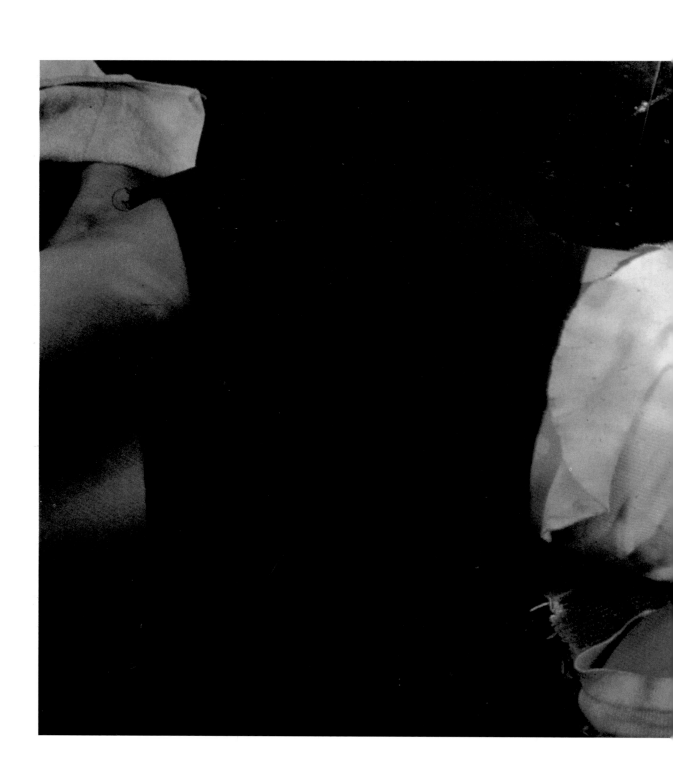

43 Untitled, #91, 1981
61 x 122 cm

44 Untitled, #97, 1982
114,3 x 76,2 cm

45 Untitled, #100, 1982
114,3 x 76,2 cm

46 Untitled, #103, 1982
76,2 x 50,2 cm

47 Untitled, #116, 1982
115 x 76,2 cm

48 Untitled, #115, 1982
115 x 76,2 cm

49 Untitled, #112, 1982
115 x 76,2 cm

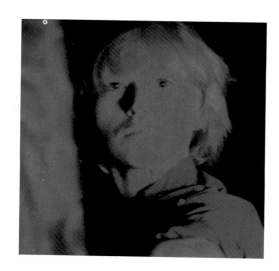

50 Untitled, #108, 1982
91 x 91 cm

51 Untitled, #109, 1982
91 x 91 cm

52 Untitled, #102, 1981
124,5 x 61 cm

53 Untitled, #122, 1983
89,5 x 54 cm

54 Untitled, #123, 1983
88,9 x 62,2 cm

55 Untitled, #300, 1994
200,7 x 134,6 cm

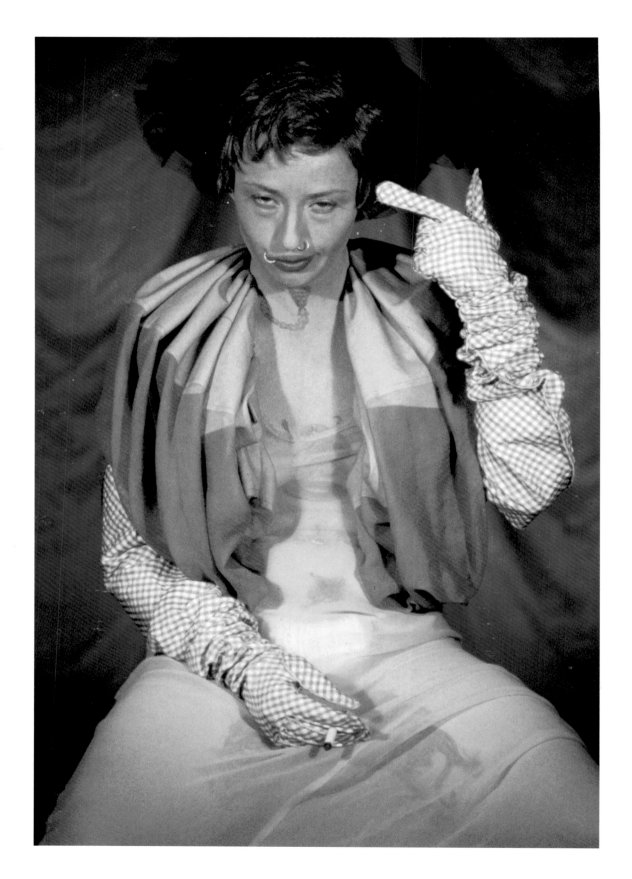

56 Untitled, #299, 1994
124,1 x 83,7 cm

57 Untitled, #119, 1983
44.5 x 91 cm

58 Untitled, #118, 1983
87.6 x 59 cm

59 Untitled, #304, 1994
155,1 x 103,9 cm

60 Untitled, #129, 1983
88,3 x 59,7 cm

61 **Untitled, #277, 1993**
124,6 x 185,4 cm

62 Untitled, #138, 1984
180,3 x 123,2 cm

63 Untitled, #133, 1984
181 x 120,7 cm

64 Untitled, #282, 1993
231,1 x 154,9 cm

65 Untitled, #298, 1994
185,4 x 125,7 cm

66 Untitled, #132, 1984
175,3 x 119,4 cm

67 Untitled, #131, 1983
88,3 x 41,9 cm

68 Untitled, #276, 1993
204,5 x 154,9 cm

69 Untitled, #205, 1989
135,9 x 102,2 cm

70 Untitled, #198, 1989
97,4 x 70,7 cm

71 **Untitled, #210, 1989**
170,2 x 114,3 cm

72 Untitled, #183, 1988
108 x 72,4 cm

73 Untitled, #228, 1990
208,3 x 121,9 cm

74 Untitled, #223, 1990
147,3 x 106,7 cm

75 Untitled, #272, 1992
67,3 x 102 cm

76 Untitled, #193, 1989
124 x 106,5 cm

77 Untitled, #216, 1989
221 x 142,2 cm

78 Untitled, #207, 1989
166,4 x 125,7 cm

79 Untitled, #222, 1990
152,4 x 111,8 cm

80 Untitled, #219, 1990
165,1 x 102 cm

81 Untitled, #141, 1985
184,2 x 125,8 cm

82 Untitled, #264, 1992
127 x 190,5 cm

83 Untitled, #152, 1985
184,2 x 124,6 cm

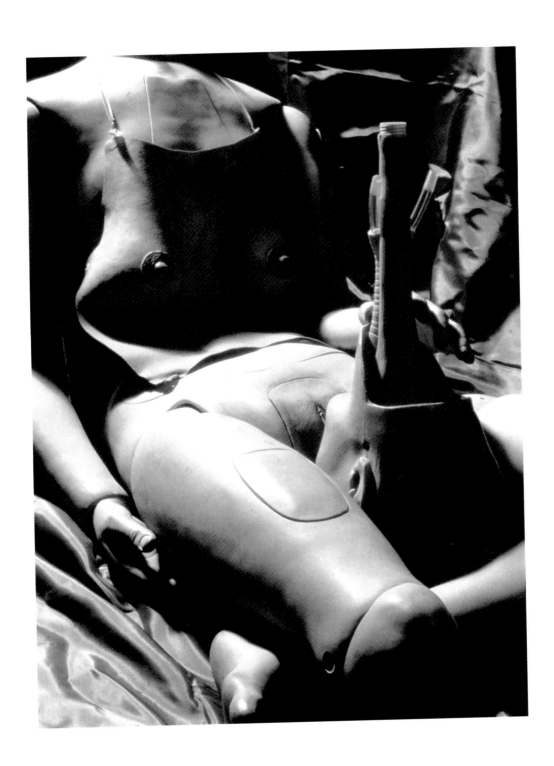

84 Untitled, #253, 1992
190,5 x 127 cm

85 Untitled, #150, 1985
125,8 x 169,5 cm

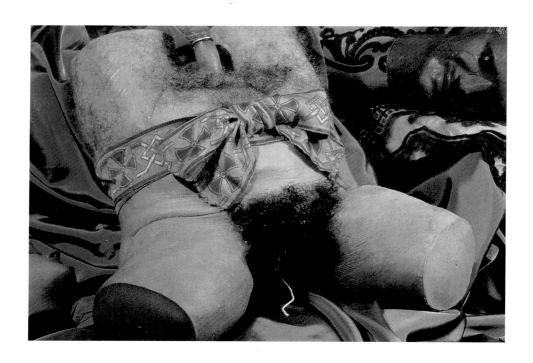

86 Untitled, #263, 1992
102 x 152,4 cm

87 Untitled, #155, 1985
184,2 x 125,1 cm

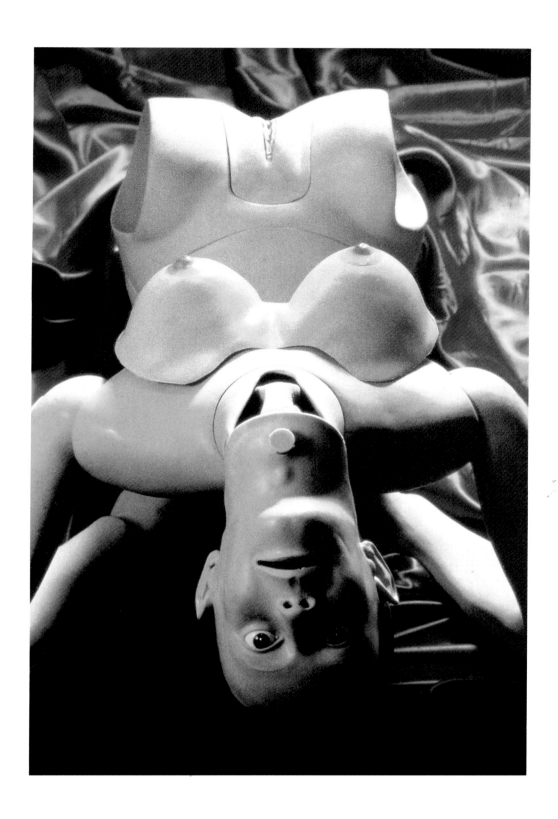

88 Untitled, #261, 1992
172,7 x 114,3 cm

89 Untitled, #146, 1985
184,2 x 124,6 cm

90 Untitled, #257, 1992
172,7 x 114,3 cm

91 Untitled, #188, 1989
109,9 x 165,1 cm

92 Untitled, #250, 1992
127 x 190,5 cm

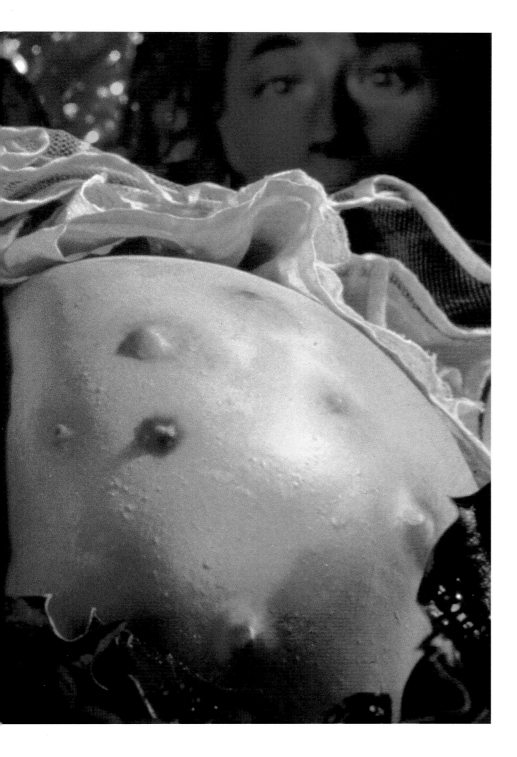

93 Untitled, #177, 1987
120,2 x 181,2 cm

94 Untitled, #190, 1989
235 x 180,3 cm

95 Untitled, #172, 1987
179,1 x 120,7 cm

96 Untitled, #175, 1987
120,7 x 179,1 cm

97 Untitled, #173, 1986
152,4 x 228,6 cm

98 Untitled, #179, 1987
179,1 x 120,7 cm

99 Untitled, #168, 1987
215,9 x 152,4 cm

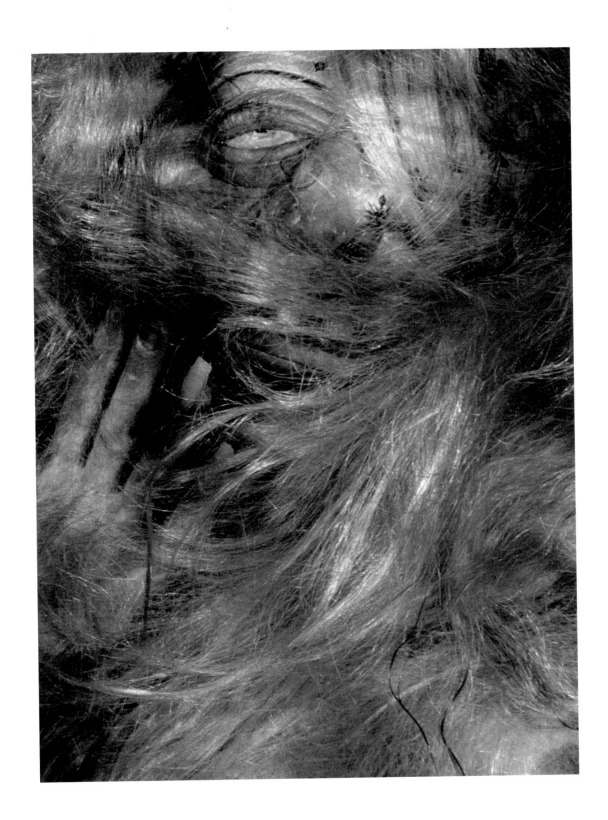

100 Untitled, #191, 1989
228,6 x 152,4 cm

101 Untitled, #140, 1985
184,2 x 124,6 cm

102 Untitled, #186, 1989
113,7 x 74,3 cm

103 Untitled, #274, 1992
67,3 x 102 cm

104 Untitled, #153, 1985
70,8 x 125,8 cm

105 Untitled, #180, 1987
243,8 x 304,8 cm

106 Untitled, #242, 1991
119,4 x 177,8 cm

107 Untitled, #243, 1991
119,4 x 177,8 cm

108 Untitled, #244, 1991
119,4 x 177,8 cm

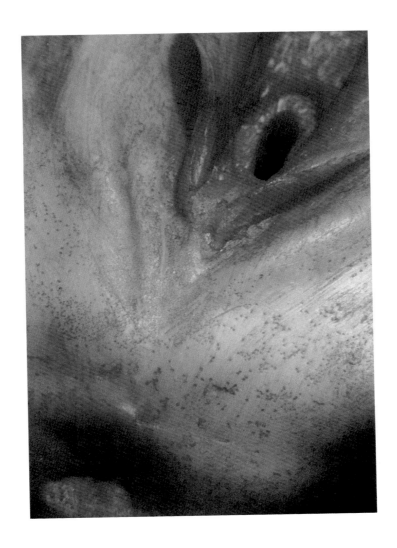

109 Untitled, #262, 1992
190,5 x 152,4 cm

110 Untitled, #311, 1994
193 x 129,5 cm

111 **Untitled, #308, 1994**
176,5 x 119,4 cm

112 Untitled, #307, 1994
200,7 x 125,7 cm

113 Untitled, #310, 1994
111,7 x 161,3 cm

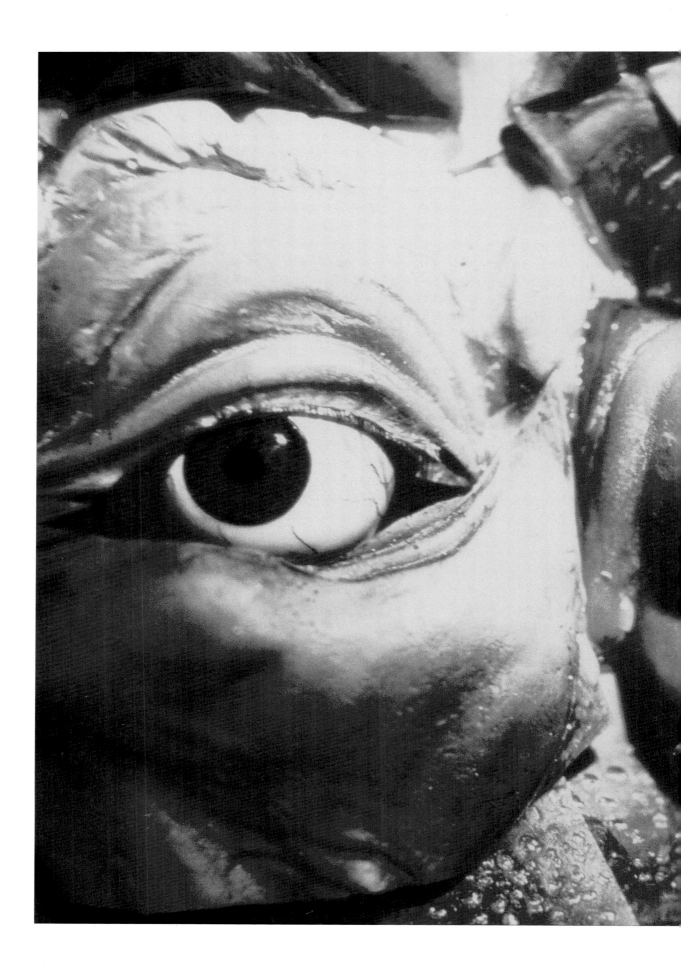

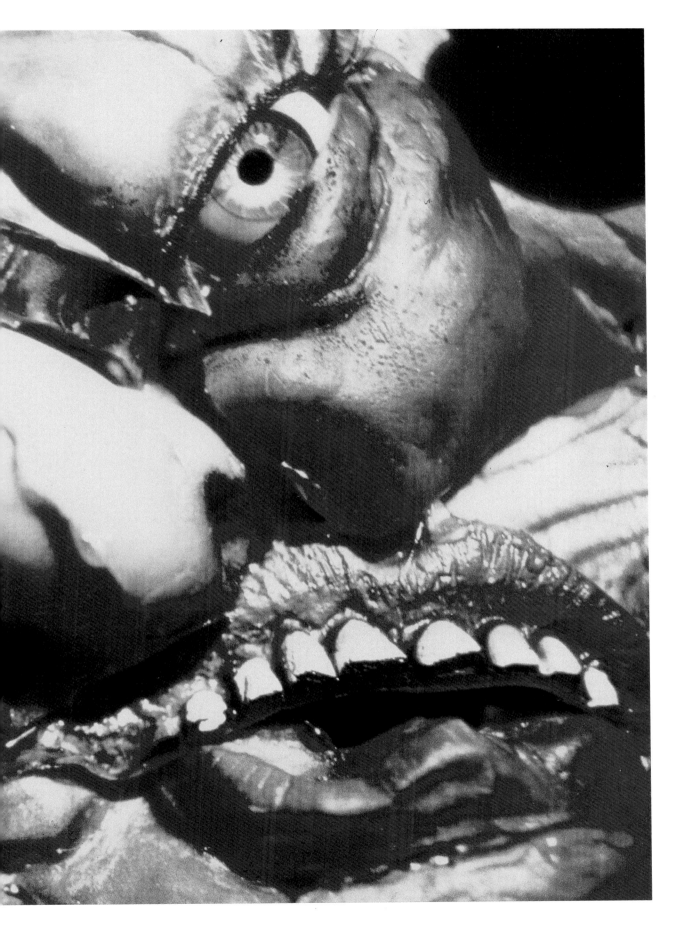

114 Untitled, #314F, 1994
76,2 x 111,7 cm

115 Untitled, #314B, 1994
111,7 x 76,2 cm

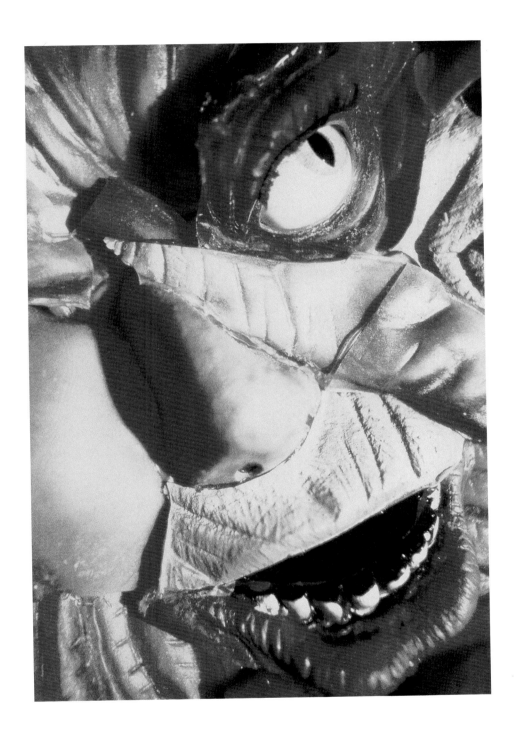

116 Untitled, #314D, 1994
111,7 x 76,2 cm

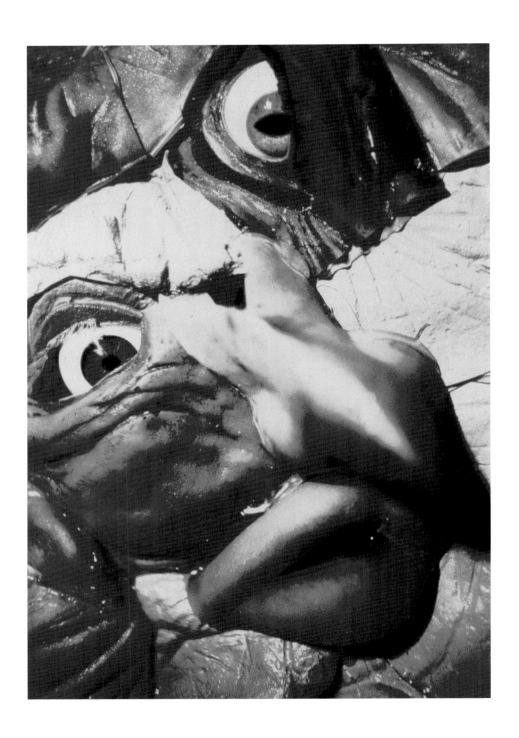

117 Untitled, #314C, 1994
111,7 x 76,2 cm

118 Untitled, #314E, 1994
111,7 x 76,2 cm

119 Untitled, #314A, 1994
76,2 x 111,7 cm

CINDY SHERMAN

Born 19 January 1954 in Glen Ridge, New Jersey.
Studied at the State University of New York in Buffalo,
New York (B.A., 1976).
Moved to New York City in 1977.

Selected One-Woman Exhibitions

1979 Hallwalls, Buffalo, New York
1980 Contemporary Arts Museum, Houston
      Metro Pictures, New York
      The Kitchen, New York
1981 Metro Pictures, New York
      Saman Gallery, Genoa, Italy
      Young/Hoffmann Gallery, Chicago
1982 Galerie Chantal Crousel, Paris
      Larry Gagosian Gallery, Los Angeles
      Metro Pictures, New York
      Texas Gallery, Houston
      Stedelijk Museum, Amsterdam; (1982–84) Gewad,
        Ghent; Watershed Gallery, Bristol; John Hansard
        Gallery, University of Southampton; Palais Stutterheim,
        Erlangen; Haus am Waldsee, Berlin; Centre d'Art
        Contemporain, Geneva; Sonja Henie-Niels Onstadt
        Foundation, Oslo; Louisiana Museum, Humlebæk,
        Denmark
1983 Fine Arts Center Gallery, State University of New York
        at Stony Brook; Zilka Gallery, Wesleyan University,
        Middletown, Connecticut
      Galerie Schellman & Klüser, Munich
      Metro Pictures, New York
      Musée d'Art et d'Industrie de Saint-Etienne
      Rhona Hoffmann Gallery, Chicago
      The St. Louis Art Museum
1984 Akron Art Museum; (1984–86) Institute of Contem-
        porary Art, Philadelphia; Museum of Art, Carnegie
        Institute, Pittsburgh; Des Moines Art Center;
        The Baltimore Museum of Art
      Monika Sprüth Galerie, Cologne
      Laforet Museum, Tokyo
      Seibu Gallery of Contemporary Art, Tokyo
1985 Metro Pictures, New York
      Westfälischer Kunstverein, Münster
1986 Galerie Crousel-Hussenot, Paris
      Portland Art Museum, Oregon
      The New Aldrich Museum, Ridgefield, Connecticut
      Wadsworth Atheneum, Hartford, Connecticut
1987 Hoffman Borman Gallery, Los Angeles
      Metro Pictures, New York
      Provinciaal Museum, Hasselt, Belgium
      Whitney Museum of American Art, New York; the
        Institute of Contemporary Art, Boston; The Dallas
        Museum of Art
1988 Galeria Comicos, Lisbon
      Galerie Lia Rumma, Naples
      Monika Sprüth Galerie, Cologne
      La Máquina Española, Madrid
1989 Galerie Crousel-Robelin, Paris
      Galerie der Wiener Sezession, Vienna
      Galerie Pierre Hubert, Geneva
      Metro Pictures, New York

National Art Gallery, Wellington, New Zealand;
  Waikato Museum of Art and History, New Zealand
1990 Monika Sprüth Galerie, Cologne
      Kunst-Station St. Peter, Cologne
      Linda Cathcart Gallery, Santa Monica
      Metro Pictures, New York
      Padiglione d'arte contemporanea, Milan
      University Art Museum, University of California,
        Berkeley
1991 Kunsthalle Basle; Staatsgalerie moderner Kunst, Munich;
        The Whitechapel Gallery, London
      Milwaukee Art Museum; Center for the Fine Arts,
        Miami; The Walker Art Center, Minneapolis
      Saatchi Collection, London
      Studio Guenzani, Milan
1992 Monika Späth Galerie, Cologne
      Galerie Six Friedrich, Munich
      Linda Cathcart Gallery, Santa Monica
      Metro Pictures, New York
      Museo de Monterrey, Mexico
1993 Galerie Ascan Crone, Hamburg
      Galerie Ghislaine Hussenot, Paris
      Galerie Susanne Ottesen, Copenhagen
      Tel Aviv Museum of Art
      Texas Gallery, Houston
      Wall Gallery, Fukuoka, Japan
      Centre Pompidou, Paris
1994 "Cindy Sherman Untitled 1987–1991", Galerie Borgman
        Capitain, Cologne
      "Cindy Sherman-New York Photographien",
        ACC Galerie, Weimar
      "Cindy Sherman-Possession", Manchester City Art
        Gallery, Manchester
      Offshore Gallery, East Hampton, New York
      "From Beyond the Pale – Cindy Sherman Photographs
        1977–1993", The Irish Museum of Modern Art, Dublin
1995 Metro Pictures, New York
      "Cindy Sherman-Photographs 1975–1995", Deichtor-
        hallen, Hamburg; Konsthall, Malmö; Kunstmuseum,
        Lucerne

Selected Group Exhibitions

1976 Albright-Knox Gallery, Buffalo, New York
      "Hallwalls", Artists' Space, New York
1977 Albright-Knox Gallery, Buffalo, New York
1978 "Four Artists", Artists' Space, New York
1979 "Re-Figuration", Max Protech Gallery, New York
1980 "Ils se disent peintres, ils se disent photographes",
        Musée d'Art Moderne, Paris
      "Likely Stories", Castelli Graphics, New York
      "Opening Group Exhibition", Metro Pictures, New York
1981 "Autoportraits", Centre Pompidou, Paris
      "Body Language: Figurative Aspects of Recent Art",
        Hayden Gallery, Massachusetts Institute of Technology,
        Cambridge; (1982–83) Fort Worth Art Museum;
        University of South Florida, Tampa; Contemporary
        Arts Center, Cincinnati
      "Erweiterte Fotografie", 5. Wiener Internationale
        Biennale, Wiener Sezession, Vienna
      "Il Gergo Inquieto", Museo Sant' Agostino, Genoa, Italy
      "Photo", Metro Pictures, New York

167

"Young Americans", Allen Memorial Art Museum, Oberlin, Ohio

1982 "Art and the Media", The Renaissance Society, University of Chicago

"Body Language", Massachusetts Institute of Technology, Cambridge

"Documenta 7", Kassel, Germany

"Eight Artists", The Anxious Edge", Walker Art Center, Minneapolis

"La Biennale di Venezia", Venice

"Lichtbildnisse: Das Portrait in der Photographie", Rheinisches Landesmuseum, Bonn

"New Figuration in America", Milwaukee Art Museum

"The Image Scavengers: Photography", Institute of Contemporary Art, Philadelphia

"20th Century Photographs from the Museum of Modern Art", Seibu Museum of Art, Tokyo, University of Hawaii Art Gallery, Honolulu

"Urban Kisses", Institute of Contemporary Art, London

1983 "Back to the U.S.A.", Kunstmuseum, Lucerne; (1983–84) Rheinisches Landesmuseum, Bonn; Württembergischer Kunstverein, Stuttgart

"Big Pictures by Contemporary Photographers", The Museum of Modern Art, New York

"Directions 1983", Hirshhorn Museum, Washington D.C.

"Drawings, Photographs", Leo Castelli Gallery, New York

"1983 Biennial Exhibition", Whitney Museum of American Art, New York

"The New Art", The Tate Gallery, London

1984 "Alibis", Centre Pompidou, Musée d'Art Moderne, Paris

"Color Photographs: Recent Acquisitions", The Museum of Modern Art, New York

"Content: A Contemporary Focus, 1974–1984", Hirshhorn Museum, Washington D.C.

"La Narrativa International de Hoy", Museo Rufino Tamayo, Mexico City; (1985) P.S. I, New York

"The Heroic Figure", Contemporary Arts Museum, Houston; (1984–85) Brooks Memorial Art Gallery, Memphis; Alexandria Museum, Alexandria, Louisiana; The Santa Barbara Museum of Art, Santa Barbara, California

"The Fifth Biennale of Sydney-Private Symbol: Social Metaphor", Art Gallery of New South Wales, Sydney, Australia

"Umgang mit der Aura", Städtische Galerie, Regensburg

1985 "Anniottanta", Galleria Comunale d'Arte Moderna, Bologna, Italy

"Autoportrait à l'époque de la photographie", Musée Cantonal des Beaux-Arts, Lausanne; Württembergischer Kunstverein, Stuttgart

"Carnegie International", Museum of Art, Carnegie Institute, Pittsburgh

"Eau de Cologne", Monika Sprüth Galerie, Cologne

"1985 Biennial", Whitney Museum of American Art, New York

"New York 85", ARCA Centre d'Art Contemporain, Marseilles

"Self-Portrait", The Museum of Modern Art, New York

1986 "Altered Egos: Samaras, Sherman, Wegman", Phoenix Art Museum, Phoenix, AZ

"Art and its Double: a New York Perspective", Fundacio Caixa de Pensions, Barcelona and La Caixa de Pensions, Madrid

"Eva und die Zukunft", Hamburger Kunsthalle, Hamburg

"Individuals: a Selected History of Contemporary Art, 1945–1986", Museum of Conteporary Art, Los Angeles

"Jenny Holzer/Cindy Sherman", The Contemporary Arts Center, Cincinnati

"La Magie de l'Image", Musée d'Art Contemporain de Montréal

"Prospect 86", Frankfurter Kunstverein, Frankfurt

"Staging the Self: Self-Portrait Photography 1840s–1980s", National Portrait Gallery, London; Plymouth Arts Centre; John Hansard Gallery, Southampton; Ikon Gallery, Birmingham

"Stills: Cinema and Video Transformed", Seattle Art Museum, Seattle

"The American Exhibition", The Art Institute of Chicago

1987 "Avant-Garde in the Eighties", Los Angeles County Museum of Art

"Implosion: a Postmodern Perspective", Moderna Museet, Stockholm

"L'Epoque, la mode, la morale, la passion: Aspects de l'art d'aujourd'hui, 1977–1987", Musée National d'Art Moderne, Centre Georges Pompidou, Paris

"Photography and Art: Interaction Since 1946", Los Angeles County Museum of Art; Museum of Art, Fort Lauderdale, Florida; Queens Museum, New York; Des Moines Art Center, Iowa

"This Is Not a Photograph: Twenty Years of Large-Scale Photography 1966–1986", The John and Mable Ringling Museum of Art, Sarasota, Florida; The Akron Art Museum, Ohio; The Chrysler Museum, Norfolk, Virginia

1988 "Matris", Konsthall, Malmö

"Presi per Incantamento", Padiglione d'Arte Contemporanea di Milano, Milan

Studio Guenzani, Milan (with Louise Lawler)

"Visions/Revisions: Contemporary Representation", Marlborough Gallery, New York

1989 "A Forest of Signs: Art in the Crisis of Representation", The Museum of Contemporary Art, Los Angeles

"Bilderstreit", Messehallen, Cologne

"Image World: Art and Media Culture", Whitney Museum of American Art, New York

"Invention and Continuity in Contemporary Photography", The Metropolitan Museum of Art, New York

"Making their Mark: Women Artists Move into the Mainstream, 1970–85", Cincinnati Art Museum; New Orleans Museum of Art; Denver Art Museum; Pennsylvania Academy of the Fine Arts, Philadelphia

"Moskau-Wien-New York", Wiener Festwochen, Vienna

"Peinture Cinéma Peinture", Centre de la Vieille Charité, Musée de Marseille, Marseilles

"Photography Now", The Victoria and Albert Museum, London

"Surrogate Selves", The Corcoran Gallery of Art, Washington D.C.

"Tenir l'image à distance", Musée d'Art Contemporain de Montréal

"The Art of Photography: 1839–1989", The Museum of Fine Arts, Houston; Ministry of Culture of the Soviet Union; Royal Academy of Arts, London

"The Photography of Invention: American Pictures of the 1980s", National Museum of American Art, Smithsonian Institution, Washington D.C.

"Three Decades: the Olivier Hoffman Collection", Museum of Contemporary Art, Chicago

1990 "Affinities and Intuitions: the Gerald S. Elliot Collection of Contemporary Art", The Art Institute of Chicago

"Culture and Commentary", The Hirshhorn Museum, Washington D.C.

"Energies", Stedelijk Musuem, Amsterdam

"Figuring the Body", Museum of Fine Arts, Boston

"Fotografie", Galerie Max Hetzler, Cologne

"Louise Lawler, Cindy Sherman, Laurie Simmons", Metro Pictures, New York

"Photography Until Now", The Museum of Modern Art, New York

"The Art of Photography: 1839–1989", Sezon Museum of Art, Tokyo

"The Decade Show", The Museum of Contemporary Hispanic Art, The New Museum, and the Studio Museum of Harlem, New York

"The Readymade Boomerang", Eighth Biennial of Sydney, Australia

"To Be and Not To Be", Centre d'Art Santa Monica, Barcelona

1991 "1991 Biennal Exhibition", Whitney Museum of American Art, New York

"Metropolis", Martin Gropius-Bau, Berlin

"Places with a Past: New Site-Specific Art in Charleston", Spoleto Festival, Charleston, South Carolina

"Devil on the Stairs: Looking Back on the Eighties", Institute of Contemporary Art, Philadelphia; Newport Harbor Art Museum, Newport Beach, California

"A Visage découvert", Fondation Cartier, Jouy-en-Josas, France

"Displacements", Atlantic Center for Contemporary Art, Las Palmas

"Carroll Dunham, Mike Kelley, Cindy Sherman", Metro Pictures, New York

"Art & Art", Castello di Rivoli, Turin

"Adam and Eve", The Museum of Modern Art, Saitama, Japan

1992 "Pleasures and Terrors of Domestic Comfort", The Museum of Modern Art, New York

"More Than Photography", The Museum of Modern Art, New York

"Ars Pro Domo", Museum Ludwig, Cologne

"Post Human", Musée d'Art Contemporain, Pully/ Lausanne; Castello di Rivoli, Turin; Deste Foundation, Athens; Deichtorhallen, Hamburg; Israel Museum, Jerusalem

"Dirty Data: Sammlung Schürmann", Ludwig Forum für Internationale Kunst, Aachen, Germany

"Imagenes de Guerra", Centro Cultural Arte Contemporanea, Mexico City

"Périls et colères", Musée d'Art Contemporain de Bordeaux

"Art of the 80s", Museo d'Arte, Sezione Contemporanea, Trent, Italy

"Selected Works from the Early Eighties", K-raum Daxer, Munich

"Spielhölle Ästhetik und Gewalt", Akademie der Kunst und Wissenschaften, Frankfurt, and Grazer Kunstverein, Graz, Austria; Galerie Sylvana Lorenz, Paris

1993 "Louise Lawler, Cindy Sherman, Laurie Simmons", Kunsternes Hus, Oslo; Museum of Contemporary Art, Helsinki

"1993 Biennial Exhibition", Whitney Museum of American Art, New York

"American Art of This Century", Martin-Gropius-Bau, Berlin; Royal Academy of Art, London

"The Uncanny, Sonsbeek "93", Geementemuseum, Arnhem, Netherlands

"Commodity Image", International Center for Photography, New York; ICA, Boston

"Konstruktion Zitat", Sprengel Museum, Hanover, Germany

"Strange Hotel", Aarhus Kunstmuseum

"L'Envers des choses", Centre Georges Pompidou, Paris

"Das Bild des Körpers", Frankfurter Kunstverein, Frankfurt

"Real Sex", Salzburger Kunstverein, Salzburg

"Up in Smoke", Knoedler & Company, New York

"Network", Kunsternes Hus, Oslo

"Diskurse der Bilder: Photokünstlerische Reprisen kunsthistorischer Werke", Kunsthistorisches Museum, Vienna

1994 "Pictures of the Real World (in Real Time)", Paula Cooper Gallery, New York

"World Morality", Kunstalle, Basle

"Saturn-Phantasmen der Vollkommenheit", Salzburger Kunstverein, Salzburg

"Against All Odds: the Healing Powers of Art", The Ueno Royal Museum and the Hakone Open-Air Museum, Japan

"Body and Soul", The Baltimore Museum of Art

"Dialogue with the Other", Kunsthallen Brandts Klaedefabrik, Denmark

"Ike + de Ander – Dignity for All: Reflections on Humanity", Beurs van Berlage, Amsterdam

"Art in the Present Tense: The Aldrich's Curatorial History, 1964–1994", The Aldrich Museum of Contemporary Art, Ridgefield, Connecticut

"Das Jahrhundert des Multiple – von Duchamp bis zur Gegenwart", Deichtorhallen, Hamburg

"Jürgen Klauke-Cindy Sherman", Sammlung Goetz, Munich

"Transformers: The Art of Multiphrenia", Minnesota Museum of American Art

"Fact and Figures", Lannan Foundation, Los Angeles

"Fotografinnen der Gegenwart", Museum Folkwang, Essen, Germany

"It's How You Play the Game", Exit Art/The First World, New York

169

Bibliographical Note

Only Cindy Sherman's own publications and monographs on her work are listed below. For the extensive secondary literature on her please see the detailed bibliography – including books, reviews of exhibitions, and journal articles – in *Cindy Sherman: Arbeiten von 1975 bis 1993*, Munich: Schirmer/Mosel, 1993.

Books by Cindy Sherman

Cindy Sherman – Specimens, ed. deAk ArTRANDOM. Kyoto: Shoin International, 1991.

Fitcher's Bird. Photographs by Cindy Sherman based on the Grimm fairy tale "Fitcher's Bird". New York: Rizzoli, 1992.

Monographs

Cindy Sherman. With a text by Els Barents. Munich: Schirmer/Mosel; Stedelijk Museum, Amsterdam, 1982.

Cindy Sherman. 2nd, expanded German edition. With texts by Els Barents and Peter Schjeldahl. Munich: Schirmer/Mosel, 1984. English edition, with texts by Peter Schjeldahl and I. Michael Danoff, New York: Pantheon Books, 1984.

Cindy Sherman. 3rd, expanded German edition. With texts by Els Barents and Peter Schjeldahl. Munich: Schirmer/Mosel, 1987. English edition, with texts by Peter Schjeldahl and Lisa Phillips, exhibition catalogue for the Whitney Museum of American Art, New York, 1987.

Cindy Sherman: Untitled Film Stills. With a text by Arthur C. Danto. German edition, Munich: Schirmer/Mosel, 1990. English edition, New York: Rizzoli; London: Jonathan Cape, 1990.

Cindy Sherman. History Portraits. With a text by Arthur C. Danto. German edition, Munich: Schirmer/Mosel, 1991. English edition, New York: Rizzoli; 1991.

Cindy Sherman: Works, 1975–1993. With texts by Rosalind Krauss and Norman Bryson. English edition, New York: Rizzoli, 1993. German edition, trans. Jörg Trobitius, Munich: Schirmer/Mosel, 1993.

TV Documentary

Nobody's Here But Me. 55 min., produced by Cinecontact for the BBC and the Arts Council of England. Director: Mark Stokes. Producer: Robert Mcnab. 1995.

The publishers are grateful to the artist and her gallery, Metro Pictures, New York, and to Jenelle Reiring and Helene Weiner, in particular, for their help and friendly support in the production of this book.

The essays by Zdenek Felix and Martin Schwander as well as the Directors' Foreword were translated from the German by Michael Robertson.

Schirmer Art Books is an imprint of Schirmer/Mosel Verlag GmbH, Munich.
For trade information please contact: Schirmer Art Books, 40, Voltaire Road, London SW4 6DH
or Schirmer/Mosel Verlag, P.O. Box 401723, 80717 München, Germany
Fax 0 89/33 86 95

A CIP catalogue record for this book
is available from the British Library

Lithos: Repro Bayer, Munich
Typesetting: Design-Typo-Print, Ismaning
Printing and binding: EBS, Verona

ISBN 3-88814-809-X
A Schirmer/Mosel production